The Best Summer Programs for Teens

2016-2017

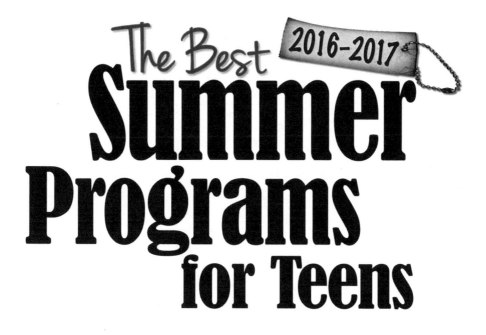

The Best 2016-2017 Summer Programs for Teens

America's Top Classes, Camps, and Courses for College-Bound Students

Sandra L. Berger

Prufrock Press Inc.
Waco, Texas

Library of Congress catalog information
currently on file with the publisher.

Edited by Katy McDowall

Cover and layout design by Raquel Trevino

ISBN-13: 978-1-61821-464-5

Printed in the United States of America.

Prufrock Press Inc.
P.O. Box 8813
Waco, TX 76714-8813
Phone: (800) 998-2208
Fax: (800) 240-0333
http://www.prufrock.com

Contents

Part I: What You Need to Know Before Choosing a Summer Program

Part II: Summer Program Directory

Part I

What You Need To Know Before Choosing a Summer Program

Introduction

There are more than 200 programs listed in *The Best Summer Programs for Teens*.

I have not visited these programs, so you will want to do some research and/or visit the programs when they are in session. I wanted to give you enough useful information so that you can look for summer programs that might be interesting and educational, and then follow through on your own. There are thousands of summer programs in the United States, so if you can't find something you like, don't give up. The universities in your area are a good resource for additional programs.

This book is written for and to students and their families. It is addressed to students and provides both information and background on topics that should interest them. Parents will be interested in the same information, but may take the most interest in the sections on paying for and choosing a program. Bright students have specific intellectual and social/emotional needs over and above other students. The programs listed in this book take account of those needs.

The program section is listed in state-by-state order, with programs listed alphabetically within each state. Each listing includes a program's contact information and a brief program description. The listings also include program websites that you can use to find further information. If the website does not answer your questions, you should write to the program at the contact information provided, and not to Prufrock Press.

Note that some of the programs have very *early deadlines*. Some fill up for the next season as soon as the program ends. So, be aware of early deadlines, especially if you need financial assistance. I hope you find something fun to do that will help you grow and prepare for your future. Happy hunting!

Chapter 1

A New Way to Look at Summer Vacation

Do you have a passion to work side by side with a microbiologist 8 hours a day? Collaborate with playwrights and directors to produce a new play? Be immersed in the world of music? Write for 12 hours a day, creating short stories, poems, essays, or a weekly newspaper? Study the ecosystems of coral reefs on daily dives in the Caribbean? Build a wooden sea kayak and paddle it along the Maine coast for 3 weeks? Go to space camp and learn from the astronauts? Learn to speak Arabic, Chinese, or Portuguese? These are all possible pursuits during the summer months.

You're probably asking yourself: Why would I go to a summer program when I could lounge poolside or hang out with my friends? Your parents are probably asking: Why would I send my child to an expensive summer program? Here's why.

The Need for Freedom to Learn Through Experience

Summer is downtime. Summer is a time for reflection and using your time in ways that are both fulfilling and fun. Somehow the schedule seems less rigid, although we may be just as busy as we are during the school year. Choosing our own activities and doing something we love makes the days and weeks fly by, especially if that something is challenging. The days are longer, giving us more daylight hours. There is the feeling of less pressure. No one is looking over your shoulder, reminding you that time is passing.

There is no other time during the year for total immersion—to immerse oneself in a self-selected activity and focus solely on that topic, to travel and meet people from other cultures, to become more linguistically, culturally, and globally aware. There is no better time to explore your interests or acquire skills that will serve you for the rest of your life. You can accelerate through an academic course with people who are as interested as you are and can work at a rapid pace. Or, you can explore a new topic not taught in school, such as archaeology or paleontology, which might ultimately lead to a college major or career. You can spend the summer learning about performing arts or computer animation. The structure and pace are yours to choose.

The learning that takes place during the summer is special. You can choose to take intellectual risks, to play with ideas, to write prose or poetry, to ask questions, to be in tune with nature. You can look at history in new ways or solve problems in new situations. There's a certain amount of risk attached to trying new things, digging into the unknown, and playing with ideas. It's risky to stretch yourself, reaching higher than you thought you could go. You might become a more interesting person. Summer is special. It's a gift of time during which you can transform yourself by building on your strengths and developing new ones. It's an opportunity to be part of an in-depth, concentrated learning experience of whatever you choose. And, if you plan ahead, you can spend the summer with people who are interested in the same activities and who have a passion for learning and sharing.

If you ask an adult about pleasant childhood memories, many will talk about one particular summer that made learning fun—a once-in-a-lifetime experience. When I was 16, I spent 9 weeks camping with a group across the United States, going to climbing school in the Rocky Mountains, learning how to recover an upended canoe in the Ely River, horseback riding along a trail, watching a beautiful sunset in the Grand Teton Park, and sailing a schooner from Bellingham, WA, to Victoria, Canada. I learned about the country, about my fellow teenage travelers, and most importantly, I learned about myself. In addition, I acquired the skills to survive in the outdoors by myself and felt more independent than when I left home.

Summer programs help us learn about communal living, acquire skills that will serve us for many years, participate in challenging courses that are paced for rapid learners, accelerate through courses that might otherwise be boring, focus on one area for weeks at a time, and take the time to think about what new areas might interest us. During the summer, in an appropriate course or program, there are opportunities for intellectual problem solving. There are countless opportunities for an exciting experience.

The Need for Advanced Instruction

Students who study music or the arts require early and advanced lessons in order to develop their full potential. The same is true of students who have talents in academic subjects like science and mathematics. These students need mentors who can answer their questions and an intellectual peer group that can stimulate their thinking. The peer group has its own energy and is sometimes just as important as the teaching. The need for advanced learning simply cannot be fulfilled during the school year. Even the most energetic teacher can't spend enough time with students who have a thirst for learning.

During the summer months, students can start building a résumé that will be essential if they aspire to apply to a highly selective college. This book includes summer programs that are not only highly selective, but also are considered essential to a growing scientist's repertoire. Programs such as Telluride in New York and ASM Materials Camp in Ohio (free to eligible students), or the Ross Mathematics Program at Ohio State University, are rigorous and offer a peer group to advanced students. These rigorous courses signal a university admissions office that a student is competitive, has an advanced knowledge base, and is ready to take on college-level work. Keep in mind that some universities listed offer space (e.g., housing and food service) to summer programs for teens, but the university does not necessarily sponsor them.

The Need for Downtime and Balance

During the academic semester, most teens lead a very hectic life, trying to fit extracurricular activities in a calendar that is already loaded with high-powered courses. Their calendars present an intimidating display of appointment dates and times. They are offended when adults tell them they are doing too much. Summer is a great time to try out new activities that you don't have time for during the school year. Just getting away from the normal day-to-day structure provides opportunities to explore and imagine. New activities and a change of pace can help you develop untried skills and expand your ideas about who you are and what you can accomplish. This is particularly important for college-bound teens, because when you look at college applications, you will find that one of the things colleges want to know is, "What are your strengths and what have you accomplished?" The question may be difficult to answer, because we don't often think about our strengths or weak areas. Summer enrichment programs present an opportunity for self-discovery, where you can test yourself and have fun with new challenges in an environment where no one is judging you and pressure is minimized. You can afford to put less pressure on yourself and be less perfectionistic than you are during the school year. The goal during the summer should be to enjoy what you are doing—to enjoy life.

The Need for Adventure and Exploration

Middle school students in particular crave adventure. If you are a middle school student, you may be interested in the protection of natural resources and the recycling of waste. You may be concerned about the decrease in population of white polar bears or whales. This does not mean that you feel self-confident in the outdoors. Many preteens and teens are intensely interested in global warming, but may actually be uncomfortable around nonpoisonous snakes, bugs, spiders, raccoons, plants they don't recognize, etc. Programs like Keystone Mountain Adventures and the Green River Preserve Summer Camp and Expeditions are perfect for students in middle school and high school. Adventure activities can include rock climbing, kayaking, mountain biking, rappelling, caving, climbing wall, SCUBA diving, and whitewater rafting. Some students are reluctant to participate in these activities, so one of the goals is to learn from experts how to be safe when you are in the wild. When you were younger, you may have enjoyed academic activities and games and spent free time indoors. You preferred Sudoku to soccer, and reading to rafting or rock climbing. You identify yourself as someone who loves to think and solve problems. The importance of spending free time doing what you love cannot be overemphasized, but at some point it's important to spend time doing activities that are unfamiliar and challenging. So, if you are one of those teens who thinks that a hike in the woods is not cool, you may want to find outdoor activities that offer environmental awareness and get to know what nature offers. In doing so, you might develop strengths that you were not aware of. It's time to stretch into a stronger you!

The Need for Enrichment and Acceleration

During the next few years, you may want to accelerate in one subject—usually math or a foreign language—or learn something entirely new like psychology, creative writing, archaeology, or genealogy. You may want to take these courses with friends who read and comprehend quickly, especially if you spend a lot of time in classes waiting for others to catch up. A typical school day divided into 55-minute segments does not leave time for pursuing courses that are not typically taught in school, exploring a topic in depth, or playing with ideas. Teachers are responsible for testing, as well as subject matter, and many are not even given time for planning. Lots of bright students do not know how to take tests, but teaching kids to take tests is just not an option. Teachers must follow a state-approved syllabus, which can be very confining. Your teachers may not have time to make courses interesting or exciting. When some of your school classes lack energy or are just plain boring, finding an appropriate summer enrichment or acceleration opportunity might be one way to relight your intellectual fire. Another might be to take courses online from an accredited school or university.

There are literally hundreds of places to look for enrichment. Your own school system is an excellent resource for finding appropriate summer programs. The cost of school-sponsored enrichment may be more reasonable than the cost of private programs. You can find these courses by calling your school system's Office of Instruction and asking about summer courses. Some school systems ask the city's Department of Parks and Recreation or Adult Education to sponsor credit courses. Do you live near a university? Most states have at least one university that offers enrichment to students during the summer. The four regional talent search programs offer academic acceleration and enrichment at the Center for Talented Youth (CTY) at Johns Hopkins University in Maryland, the Talent Identification Program (TIP) at Duke University in North Carolina, the Center for Bright Kids (CBK) Regional Talent Development Center in Colorado, and the Center for Talent Development (CTD) at Northwestern University in Illinois. Between these four talent searches, students throughout the entire United States have access to talent identification services, publications, and educational programs, including enrichment. Additional programs are listed in this book. Honors and Advanced Placement courses are typically accelerated—that is, presented in half the number of hours as scheduled by a normal school semester.

The Need for Independence

Young people need a variety of experiences, especially during the teen years. Most teens also want and need to lessen their dependence on their parents, form separate identities, and stand on their own feet. Summer is the ideal time for learning responsible ways of becoming independent; camp or some other summer activity provides a wholesome escape from home, school, friends, and expectations. Kids have the freedom to be themselves in an environment that is more flexible and offers a change of pace and context. There are many different types of summer activities where you will have a good time and learn something new or improve a favorite activity. This book, for students and parents, is a guide to programs that emphasize learning opportunities of all types. These opportunities have one thing in common—they are designed for preteens or teens and there is something for everyone.

Growth in Self-Esteem

Based on research, we know that students who were accelerated in mathematics at an early age experienced an increase in self-esteem that was directly related to the acceleration. This effect of acceleration has been seen across many academic disciplines (Davidson & Davidson, 2004; McClarty, 2015). Attending an appropriate summer program that provides acceleration is one way for college-bound students to gain academic self-confidence. Moving through a course at your own pace is empowering socially as well as emotionally. Rapidly paced summer programs can give you a feeling of accomplishment and increased control over your life. We also know that when teens research summer programs, decide with their families how and where they want to spend the summer months, take responsibility for planning and preparing, and, finally, earn some or all of the money to pay for it, the end result is growth-promoting. If you succeed in doing something you were not sure you could do, you are likely to see yourself in a new light. Your parents will appreciate your growing independence and sense of responsibility.

It may be important to tell your parents that children who attended a summer program where they found friends like themselves and interesting activities say that they benefited in many ways, including (American Camp Association, 2005):

- growth in confidence and increased self-esteem,
- ability to make new friends,
- growth of independence and leadership skills, and
- willingness to try new things and participate in adventurous activities.

Learning Through Summer Experiences

Communal Living

If you are planning to spend your summer in a residential program, you will be part of a large community, perhaps on a university campus. Communal living is quite unlike living with your family. In communal living, you are more independent than you are at home, most of the choices you make have a direct impact on your peer group, and you are responsible for those choices. At home, if you are not tidy, your parents may remind you to pick up your things. Living away from home, your group is not likely to be so courteous. There are negative consequences if you don't treat members of your group well. Cooperation is one of the first things teens learn when living with other teens. Kids meet new challenges and conquer fears with peer group support and a sense that they belong to a community.

Career Testing and Building

If you are thinking about careers, like most college-bound students, this is the perfect time to do some testing and experimenting. Summer is a great time to start building credentials that will later open the door to new opportunities. When you apply to colleges, you will be asked about your interests and passions. If you can show that your interests began when you were young and have developed over time (establishing a track record), if you have participated in competitions or shown some leadership in your interest areas, you will lay the groundwork for building credentials. (We'll say more about credentials in the next chapter of this book.)

For example, a student whom we'll call Isabel wanted to go into broadcasting. She thought she had some of the necessary people skills and loved the idea of appearing in front of a camera. Isabel and her mother went to a local television station so Isabel could look for volunteer opportunities. She persuaded a producer to give her an opportunity as an intern, and worked there all summer. She learned about life behind the scenes and discovered that broadcasting was a lot less glamorous than she imagined. This experience served her well, and she took advantage of other opportunities to volunteer in similar places. When Isabel applied to college, because of her experiences, she had decided her major and knew that she wanted to enter the field of advertising. She had the background to persuade the college to accept her application and offer some financial aid.

Another student, Karl, was really good at mathematics and knew that he wanted to take calculus and statistics in high school. He also knew that 4 years of high school did not give him time to do everything that interested him. So, Karl took algebra during the summer after seventh grade and made sure that he had the documentation that his high school required to give him credit. He took geometry during the summer after eighth grade. By the time he reached 11th grade, he was able to take advanced math courses at the local college.

There are many students like Karl who, for a variety of reasons, want to accelerate through middle and high school, particularly in subjects they are good at. By using the summer months during middle school, they set the stage for doing just that. Just as you would try several pairs of shoes to see which is the best fit, trying on a career for size will make you most comfortable later on. For advanced students, summer can be a rich gold mine of opportunities, whether you are taking academic courses, acquiring leadership skills, traveling, helping those less fortunate by volunteering, working in a laboratory like the one at the Naval Observatory, participating in research, honing athletic skills, or getting involved in the arts. The right summer program can become part of the architecture of your life.

Getting Credit

Some students accelerate by taking out-of-school courses they would normally take during the school year. There are many summer academic courses that will grant either high school or college credit. However, many high schools will not accept credit earned in a summer program not sponsored by your school district. Some high schools will not place an accelerated student in the next course in the sequence. For example, if you take algebra or geometry and excel, it's reasonable to expect that in the fall, you will be able to sign up for the next math course in the sequence. What is reasonable to expect may be counter to your school district's policy. Many schools are concerned about their offerings when a student has accelerated and finishes an academic sequence as a sophomore or junior. The instructional staff may fear being pressured to offer advanced courses for only a few students by a limited teaching staff. Thus, schools may discourage students from taking out-of-school courses because of the long-term consequences. Because this is not uncommon, you must discuss the consequences with your school before your family spends a lot of money on a summer course. If you and your parents want to try convincing your school district that acceleration works, a publication and website that provides significant research can be found at http://www.accelerationinstitute.org.

Perhaps you can get the courses you need online, through either a university or one of the talent search programs mentioned earlier. Although I would not recommend this path, it may be helpful to know that many universities will enroll young students with no high school diploma if the student can prove that he or she is capable of college-level work. You can accomplish this by taking a few online courses at a local college. The other thing you should know is that colleges are less enthusiastic than they used to be about AP courses, and some will give credit or placement only to those who have scored a 5 on an AP test.

Chapter 2

College Planning: Take a Dry Run This Summer

Enrolling in a residential academic summer program that takes place on a college campus will give you a taste of college life. Think of it as a dry run that will expose you to pathways that are helpful and hazards to avoid. You will get the feel of a college campus as a community. You will live in a dormitory with other students, eat with them in the dining hall, and use the campus library. On your way to the dining hall or library, read the notices on the wall. Are students passionate about politics? Do they care about the same things that you care about? Read the college newspaper. Most campuses have wireless networks and connecting your personal computer is simple. But also check to see if there are computer labs, especially if you are interested in computer programming. If you think you might be a science major, visit the science labs when students are there. Check to see how many students use each microscope or other equipment and ask who teaches the lab courses. Of course, there is more to school than classes, so be sure to check out the weekend scene. Where is the nearest theater with first-run movies or popular music concerts? At some schools, students must find transportation to the nearest town to see a movie. But, in some cases, they are not allowed to have cars until sophomore or junior year and there is no public transportation. If that makes a big difference to you and you would not want to be in that position, you have learned something about yourself, as well as something to look for at other colleges. When you select colleges to apply to, you will have an advantage if you have lived on different types of campuses during the summer. You will know what and who to look for and how to orient yourself.

Eventually you will need to figure out the differences and similarities among different types of colleges and universities (e.g., small private liberal arts, technical schools, teaching/research universities, large state universities) and decide where you feel most comfortable. How is Cal Tech different from MIT, the University of Michigan, or North Carolina State University? If you want a career in technology or engineering, it's a good idea to figure out how the programs at those four schools differ from one another. College courses are different than high school courses in many ways. First, in college you have more choices. You can choose not to go to class and deal with the consequences. Second, someone—either you or your parents—has paid for the courses. Teachers are different. In high school, your teachers know who you are and will applaud your efforts. On a large campus with large classes, faculty members may not have a clue about you. If you get to know them, it will be because you made an effort. If you like anonymity, that can be an advantage. But, if you need to like a teacher in order to make good grades, check out a smaller campus environment. Some colleges have tutorial classes and seminars for freshman students. Some colleges offer a trimester system where you can study fewer courses for a shorter period of time. The end result in credits earned is the same as the more typical system where you take five courses each semester, but students have more time to focus on each course or topic. While you are on campus for a summer residential program, talk to students and ask what they liked and disliked about their courses and experiences. At a later time, you might talk to professionals in the field that interests you to ask which college courses were most useful and which were a total waste of time.

Selectivity

Selectivity is an issue for all college applicants. It has to do with the ratio of the number of applicants to a specific college versus the number of students accepted and by extension, the rigor of the courses. A university that accepts one student out of every 10 or 15 applicants is highly selective. Harvard, Princeton, Yale, MIT, and most of the Ivy League schools (called "Ivies") are all highly selective. Selectivity is one of the most important factors in choosing a college because it tells you what your acceptance chances are and, if enrolled, how hard you will have to work. A highly selective school is likely to attract highly competitive students. For years, the ratio of applicants to acceptances (e.g., 10 applicants to 1 accepted) was the best way to assess the level of challenge. Since 2000, however, there is a different method to assess schools, developed by the National Survey of Student Engagement (NSSE). Its website is http://nsse.indiana.edu.

NSSE asked students 30 questions about their classes, such as "How often did you prepare two or more drafts of a paper?" The answers fall in a range from *very often* to *never*. Looking at the survey, you will quickly see that students who take rigorous, challenging classes are going to answer one way and students who take easy classes will answer an entirely different way. The survey was not developed for this use, so you may be wondering how this helps you look at colleges. First, the survey responses for each school give you the level of challenge. Second, the survey responders were students who had to gauge the rigor of their courses. This method of gauging the rigor of courses is a lot more accurate than information provided in the many college handbooks on the market. There are other college guides that provide student responses to questions about their school, but they do not look at the courses and level of challenge. For example, to compile *The Best 379 Colleges*, the Princeton Review asked more than 130,000 college students what their schools were really like. The "Best Party School" ranking list gets a lot of attention, but it is just one small part of this guide. Its survey is available at the following website: http://www.princetonreview.com/college-rankings.aspx.

If you are thinking about applying to a selective college or university, the way you spend your summers is extremely important. Colleges want to know that you have chosen your summer activities wisely, developed your talents, and achieved success in highly rigorous courses. Experience is empowering. The more experiences you have, the better you will know what you can easily do and which activities are challenging. This may sound simplistic, but it's not. Learning about yourself—your limits, as well as your successes—is ongoing and very complex, but it can be fun.

If you aspire to a highly selective college, the following factors might give you an edge over equally competitive students. You may think you don't need an edge, but there are more than 27,000 valedictorians each year. What if all or most of them wanted to attend the same college that interests you? Would your résumé boost you to the top of the application pile?

- *Track Record (Long-Time Interest Leading to True Expertise):* This is where summer programs count the most. College admissions faculty are not going to be impressed if you do 10 or 12 things during high school. They are looking for activities that continued over several years. So, if you are interested in marine science, global warming, or oceanology, it is very important to spend your summers learning all you can from a variety of resources. Field research is particularly important. Woods Hole Oceanographic Institution in Massachusetts states prominently on its website:

  > Preparation for a career in oceanography should begin as early as possible with a concentration in one scientific discipline. In high school, you should plan your studies around college-preparatory courses including math, English, science, and foreign languages. In college, you should choose a basic field of science in which to earn your first academic degree. ("Marine Careers," 2014, ¶ 1)

- *Suitable Program Matching Student Goals*: Colleges want to see a match between your interests and goals and their offerings. For example, if your ultimate goal is a career in international business and you can show the different ways that you have become interested in the field—internships, volunteering, etc.—and if the college of your choice has an outstanding economics department, you have probably found a way to make yourself stand out as an applicant. However, keep in mind that there is a difference between padding your résumé and engaging in activities because you have passion. Admission officers are trained to spot extracurricular activities that look good on your college application but don't really add anything substantive.
- *Compelling Need (A Unique Need Only You Can Fill)*: Colleges want to know how applicants will make a unique contribution to the school. For example, if you are a published poet and the school is known for its creative writing courses, you might be considered a "compelling" applicant. No one can tell you how to become a compelling applicant. That story can be written only by you.
- *Clear Goals*: If it is clear that your summers are part of a master plan, your career goals can give you an edge, particularly if those goals are demonstrated by a track record.
- *Prestige*: Ivies pride themselves on names and contributors. This is out of your control unless you have a huge trust fund. Do *not* get a letter of recommendation from an important person who doesn't know you well. *Do* get a letter of recommendation from one of the mentors you cultivated during summer activities, especially if that person knows your work well and can speak to your potential success.
- *Special Qualities:* Awards or competitions (e.g., Intel Science Talent Search), atypical career goals (e.g., male nurses), talent areas (e.g., playing the bagpipes, bassoon, or oboe). One selective college offers a scholarship to academically qualified students who can successfully audition for its competitive "pipe band" or who want to compete with its team

of Highland dancers or drummers. Summer experiences help with these special qualities because they give an eligible candidate a boost. For example, if math is your passion, your participation in the Ross Mathematics Program (http://www.math.osu.edu/ross) will make you stand out when you apply to colleges. If you are interested in intellectual challenge and have a passion for learning, the Telluride Association's sophomore (TASS) and junior (TASP) programs offer a summer educational experience with "challenges and rewards rarely encountered in secondary school or even college" ("What Is TASP?" n.d., ¶ 1).

- *A Contribution to the School*: Yale University displays prominently on its website: "As we carefully and respectfully review every application, two questions guide our admissions team: 'Who is likely to make the most of Yale's resources?' and 'Who will contribute most significantly to the Yale community?'" ("What Yale Looks For," n.d., ¶ 2). When you think about summer activities, it is important to enjoy yourself and to connect the experience to your personal growth by asking, "Why do I want to attend this program?"

Bolster Test-Taking Skills

How are your test-taking skills? If you are in middle school (seventh or eighth grade), it's a good idea to take the SAT or ACT. Your scores on either test may give you acceptance to a regional talent search program and the fast-paced courses they offer. These courses also offer a peer group of youngsters who enjoy intellectual pursuits. Younger students, grades 2 through 6, gain admission to talent search programs by taking the SCAT test. Most precollege academic summer programs want to see your PSAT/SAT/ACT scores when you submit an application. Typically, eligible students have scored at levels comparable to college-bound seniors.

If you are planning to take the PSAT/NMSQT (Preliminary Scholastic Assessment Test/National Merit Scholarship Qualifying Test) in 10th grade, you should spend some time becoming familiar with the test. The NMSQT is the qualifying test for becoming a National Merit Finalist and winning a scholarship if your 11th-grade scores are high enough. The PSAT/NMSQT is practice for the real SAT, which many students will need to take in order to apply for college. The scores don't count until 11th grade and you can learn a lot in a year, especially if you know the areas where you are weak. Some very bright students are terrible test takers, especially on standardized timed tests. Although poor test-taking skills isn't the end of the world, it's important to score high enough on these tests so that you don't become ineligible for programs and colleges that use standardized test scores as a criterion for admission. Schools that receive many thousands of applications sometimes make the first cut based on test scores. They use the average of your grade point average, class rank, and standardized test scores. You will want to make sure your scores are high enough that you aren't eliminated immediately. If you are a poor test taker because you have a learning disability, there's a book you should look at: *Rock the SAT* by Michael Moshan, David Mendelsohn, and Michael Shapiro, and published by McGraw-Hill in 2006. The authors have structured the book around 13 songs they wrote for learning vocabulary. They believe that vocabulary is where students get hung up and that it's much easier to learn vocabulary to music (as opposed to flash cards). The vocabulary words chosen for the book are, according to the authors, the most commonly used words in the SAT. Another good study skills book for students with learning disabilities is *Becoming a Master Student* by Dave Ellis (2014).

SATs and ACTs: To Prep or Not to Prep

If taking a prep course will boost your scores, do it! The average increase, according to instructors, is at least 100 points. You can increase your scores that much by knowing test-taking tricks. It's reasonable to take the SAT or ACT three times, once during middle school and twice during high school. However, three times should be your limit. Beyond that, it's really a waste of your time, because you are not likely to increase your score enough to make a big difference to the colleges. The exception is using a test prep program. If you have taken the test twice in high school and your scores do not reflect your ability and knowledge, by all means take a good prep course. There are several websites where you can take practice tests and one site where you can take a free preparation course (https://www.march2success.com). If you have severe test anxiety, you should definitely take some kind of prep course at a time when you can focus and give it some attention—summer. Choose a course where the instructor will analyze your test results and tell you specifically how you can raise your scores.

College Application Prep Camps

Did you know that there are a growing number of traditional and academic summer camps that will prepare students for the college application process? Most of these camps are located on college campuses so you can glimpse a peek of campus life while you are there. Campers spend their time working on SAT or ACT preparation, academic workshops where you can bolster your strengths and work on your weaknesses, essay writing, mock admissions interviews, and other parts of the process. Some camps will give advice on specific colleges, depending on where the staff attended college. Campers are usually rising seniors who want to get a jump on the process. These camps are expensive and many people believe there are better ways to spend your summer, but if you decide such a camp is right for you, you may find such programs by conducting an online search for "college admission prep camp."

Summer Activities Say Something About You

When you complete college applications, the college will want to know who you are. Your grades and standardized test scores say one thing about you. Your extracurricular activities fill in the picture somewhat. But colleges want to know what you are passionate about. They want to see a documentation of activities where you have honed your skills and some evidence that you can persevere. Colleges want to see commitment. They want to see leadership. When admissions officers sit down to look at an overwhelming pile of applications, they may give each applicant 5 or 10 minutes during the first run through. At that point, they divide applications into three piles—yes, no, and maybe. At the very least, you want to wind up in the maybe pile. You will need some credentials to demonstrate that you can successfully work at the college level. And, if you apply to a highly selective school, you may compete against 10,000 applicants. Even if your grades and standardized test scores put you at the top of the heap, you will need something else that answers the question, "Why should I admit you to this college?"

Some people believe that telling schools how you have overcome hardship is one of the keys to getting into a selective school. It's a myth. Schools want to see the results of your efforts. If you were a Dean of Admission, you would want to see that a student loves learning, enjoys new challenges, and knows how to set goals and succeed. Resiliency and overcoming hardship certainly counts, but only if you have a host of other qualities and can make it apparent as to how you will contribute to a college community. Students who are exposed to lots of different situations and activities are more interesting than students who spend all of their time "making grades." Students who set realistic goals and gradually improve are seen as independent thinkers. Documentation counts. If you are a basement scientist, eventually you will have to test your mettle by demonstrating a project to people qualified to assess your work. If you are interested in writing, enter some contests every year and demonstrate how you have grown over time. If you can't afford a summer program, look for an online program. If you are interested in wind surfing, that is terrific, but admissions faculty will hardly be impressed unless you link wind surfing to an intense curiosity about physics, mathematics, or some other academic area and demonstrate that you are successful in those areas.

The earlier you can start planning for appropriate summer activities, the more time you will have until the end of high school. If you wait until high school, you have only three summers to learn what you can and accomplish your goals. The key is to plan ahead and understand the options.

Chapter 3

What Will You Do This Summer?

The Fast-Track Generation

If you are young, you may not be able to remember what life was like before the Internet. You may not remember long-playing or 45 rpm records. Today's teens are overprogrammed, overscheduled, and exhausted. Academic demands ratchet up as students take on more Advanced Placement courses or International Baccalaureate programs. In addition, a fast-growing, elite program is making its way to U.S. schools. The College Board's AP Capstone™ program for high school students "is an innovative diploma program that provides students with an opportunity to engage in rigorous scholarly practice of the core academic skills necessary for successful college completion" (AP Capstone™, 2015).

The fallout of taking excessive rigorous courses has, for some, come in the form of self-destructive behaviors such as eating disorders. A word of caution before we talk about programs: If you are overprogrammed and wondering if it is all worth it, staying home may not solve your problem. You may want to learn something that is purely fun, like photography, and avoid anything academically challenging during the summer. Your health is more important than your résumé.

Types of Programs

What are the connections between summer programs and college? As you look at the types of program opportunities, keep in mind that you are writing the story of *you*. The decisions you make have consequences beyond this summer, and hopefully will blend with your other choices to tell a story. So, if you tell colleges you want to major in foreign languages, taking AP language courses in high school during the regular semester makes sense. Building the story of you, during the weekends you might spend 3 hours every Saturday morning tutoring children who speak only Spanish. During the summer, if you can afford it, a trip to someplace in South America for a community service project will add additional substance to your experiences. If you can't afford travel or any other type of formal summer program, look around the city where you live for opportunities to help newly arrived immigrants to get basic services like food or education. The best way to do this is through your city's adult education or social service department. Perhaps you will be qualified to teach English or help in some other way. Summer is also a good time to find out if you *really* want to major in foreign languages. Too many adults find out too late that they are unhappy with their career choice. Consider summer a dress rehearsal and try a career on for size. Most importantly, I can't say strongly enough that you should never choose a program only because you think it will look good on your résumé or impress the admissions committee. They need to know who you are, not who you pretend to be.

This section discusses the many different types of programs and provides information on several options, including both academic and adventurous opportunities. Keep in mind that two programs of the same type may be very different. Read the "fine print" so you will know what you are getting into. I have chosen not to include athletic programs in this book. If you are an athlete, your high school coach and teammates are a great source for information about summer activities in your sport.

We'll look at the following types of programs in the sections that follow:

* travel,
* gap year,
* academic enrichment or acceleration,
* fine and performing arts,
* service learning and youth leadership programs,
* volunteer programs, and
* internships.

Travel

Summer travel programs offer you the opportunity to see some of the world, meet people from different countries, learn a new language, and live in a different culture. Travel gives you the opportunity to "try on a different you," to create that once-in-a-lifetime experience that might change your life. During college, you may have to spend summers earning money for the following academic year. So, it's possible you may not have another opportunity to travel until you have finished college. Students who participate in travel programs often say they learn as much about their own views as they do about the topics they study, the people they meet, and the places they visit.

There are two types of travel programs: short-term and year-round. Short-term programs usually last several weeks during summer or school breaks; most require an adult chaperone. Some groups are sponsored by school systems or local universities. Lodging varies, depending on the program. Some school districts sponsor short-term overseas travel that is preceded by several weeks of summer school during which teens learn about the history and language of a country. Following travel, students are debriefed and have the opportunity to exchange photos and experiences. Year-round homestay programs are meant for students who wish to stay with a family in the country that interests them, attend language classes, and attend a local school. Some programs provide opportunities for high school and college students to participate in service projects in other countries.

Homestay Programs

Many private companies specialize in sponsoring youth in different countries where they live with a host family. If travel takes place during the school semester, students have the opportunity to lead the typical day-to-day life of a high school age student in another country. It takes an open mind, a sense of humor, and flexibility to be a successful exchange student. (Keep in mind that you are not a tourist. You should not expect your homestay family to take you on a tour of the country.) However, the experiences leave students with greater confidence, maturity, and self-awareness, not to mention fluency in another language if you are there long enough and have the desire to learn.

There is much to think about if you want a homestay program, much more than this book can provide. The insurance issues are formidable, particularly because families need to find travel insurance that will offer protection if students need health or hospital care while they are abroad. For that reason, as well as others, finding a good consultant to help you select a program may save you time and confusion. One of the most important factors is the selection of a homestay family and their commitment to a visiting student. You need to make sure that if the homestay family has a change of heart because of changes in their family situation, the program will provide a carefully selected alternative family. Some organizations visit recommended host families in their homes while others use only recommendations and phone conversations. Some programs require host families to participate in an orientation, while others rely on printed material and conversations. You also will need at least one local program contact who will introduce you to your family and who knows how to proceed if there is a mismatch between you and the family. Make sure there is a solid support group in the country of your choice—people who are fluent in English, as well as the native language. As you can see, homestays are complex, which is why you would benefit from working with an independent consultant.

Summer Travel

Choosing a summer travel program is challenging. You have to decide what type of program you want, the length of your stay, where you want to live, whether you want or need high school credit, and the size of the program. Think about your goals for a travel program. Here are some questions to consider as you do your research.

- *Leadership*: Is the leader experienced? The leadership for a short-term program is particularly critical to this type of trip. Each leader must be knowledgeable about the country and language and have experience working with teenagers. Check the qualifications each program requires of its leaders.
- *Activities*: The activities vary from program to program, so read the itinerary carefully. Is enough time spent in each location to absorb some of its characteristics? Is there an extra cost for some activities?
- *Language*: The amount of time spent on language varies from program to program. Most short-term programs emphasize informal conversation and do not attempt a structured program. If perfecting a foreign language is your goal, look for a program that specializes in language study.

Some students start their search for summer travel with a particular country, but if you are not sure of what country to visit, you should check out the website of The Council on Standards for

International Educational Travel (CSIET; http://www.csiet.org). CSIET is a private, nonprofit organization whose mission is to identify reputable international youth exchange programs so that teens are provided with meaningful and safe international exchange experiences. It sets standards for foreign study programs. It evaluates exchange programs to make certain that they adhere to certain practical and safety standards, and lists all approved exchange organizations in the annual CSIET directory, the *Advisory List of International and Educational Travel and Exchange Programs*. This directory is published as a service to schools, students, and host families. The *Advisory List* provides a resource from which prospective exchange students, their parents, and school leaders can confidently glean an understanding of the scope, background, and operations of programs that have been reviewed.

If programs on the CSIET list are not suitable, choose a well-known program that will let you talk to the students who have used that service. Most organizations have at least a few parents and alumni students who are willing to talk to prospective travelers. If they won't release any names, you should move on to a different organization. Programs like The Experiment in International Living (http://www.experiment.org) have been around for a long time and its website invites interested people to contact alumni. Resources for student travel can be found in Table 1.

Gap Year Programs

Most students head to college right after high school because that's the established path. Their parents expect it, they've taken the required classes, and all their friends are going. However, an increasing number of teens contemplating 4 more years of similar academic experiences in college elect to take a "gap year," a semester or academic year off from school to travel abroad, explore a career path by working or serving an internship, or commit to a program where they can help others who are less fortunate (e.g., Habitat for

Table 1
Student Travel Resources

Council on Standards for International Educational Travel (CSIET)
http://www.csiet.org

The Experiment in International Living
http://www.experiment.org

Abbey Road Programs
http://www.goabbeyroad.com

ASPECT Foundation
http://www.aspectfoundation.org/study_abroad/index.html

Bold Earth Teen Adventures
http://boldearth.com

Deer Hill Expeditions
http://www.deerhillexpeditions.com

Where There Be Dragons
http://www.wheretherebedragons.com

World Horizons International, LLC
http://www.worldhorizons.com

ActionQuest
http://www.actionquest.com

CCI Greenheart
http://www.cci-exchange.com

Global Crossroad
http://www.globalcrossroad.com

Backroads
http://www.backroads.com

Table 1, continued

International Cultural Adventures http://www.ICAdventures.com
Williwaw Adventures http://www.williwawadventures.com
Youth for Understanding USA http://www.yfu-usa.org
American Trails West http://www.atwteentours.com
Columbia University Summer Programs for High School Students http://ce.columbia.edu/high-school
Summer Study http://www.summerstudy.com/index.cfm
Westcoast Connection Teen Travel Experiences http://www.westcoastconnection.com
Amigos de las Américas http://www.amigoslink.org
Transitions Abroad http://www.transitionsabroad.com
Volunteers for Peace (VFP) http://www.vfp.org
National Outdoor Leadership School (NOLS) http://www.nols.edu
Summerfuel http://www.summerfuel.com
University of Dallas High School Summer Programs http://www.udallas.edu/travel

Humanity). And some teens take a postgraduate year in school to prepare themselves academically for college classes.

Taking a gap year is a common practice in Europe, particularly England. This trend is growing in the United States, with many students taking time off before, during, or after college. Some highly selective colleges recommend it, understanding that bright intense students have been in an academic pressure cooker for years and need time out before jumping into a different but equally intense college experience. These colleges have found that students who take a gap year with specific goals "have it together." They return to school with renewed energy and motivation.

Students have many other reasons for taking a gap year. Those who did not get into their first choice college may want to make themselves more competitive by serving an internship or documenting their skills in a work environment. Some need to earn additional money for college, although most admissions counselors discourage students from delaying college to earn money. Anything a student earns will be counted when determining financial aid and may reduce the student's financial aid package. Some feel the urge to see some of the world before settling down to campus life. Some want the answer to the questions, "Why should I go to college?" and "What does college have to do with what I want in my life?" And, some want to contribute to a cause bigger than themselves. Whatever your reason for taking a gap year or semester, you will have to explain why you made the specific program choice and, like everything else, your reasons should be a part of writing the story of you and should be consistent with your overall goals.

The number of gap year programs and consultants is on the increase and shouldn't be difficult to find. It's far better to take a year off than to enter a professional field and suddenly realize that you are in the wrong place. This happens to adults who, all too often, say that they ended up in their profession because of someone else's expectations or that they simply drifted into it without pausing to think whether they really loved their work. Many students get into a college and attend for 2 or more years before deciding that they are in the wrong place. This is not because the college has changed.

Rather, it is because the student has changed and needs a different environment. However, transferring to a different school may cost some earned credit hours because your new school does not have to accept all of your credits. If you can structure your summers as one method to explore academic subjects and career paths, you are less likely to fall into the wrong school or wrong career trap.

If a college that you want to attend has accepted you for admission, taking a gap year requires deferral. Here is how that works: To defer, you will put down an enrollment deposit by May 1 (or thereafter if you are admitted off of a waiting list). Then, you will ask the college, in writing, to hold your place while you defer admission, usually for a full year but sometimes only for a semester.

If you did not apply to any colleges, were not admitted to any, or were admitted only to colleges in which you have no interest, then you are considering a different track: a real gap year during which you will apply (or reapply) to a full list of colleges while pursuing activities that interest you and that will improve your chances of getting in.

Taking time off may seem like a great idea when you are feeling overwhelmed with final exams, AP exams, IB program assignments, and even overwhelmed by activities you love. But trust me, you will need to think this through before deferring college. First, you will have to carefully document the reason for taking a gap year. Backpacking across Europe sounds exciting, but unless you are a language major or passionate about intercultural studies, spending a year in a country to visit and backpack might not convince an admissions committee to defer your admission. Whatever you choose, be prepared to defend your choice. Keep a diary, because if you try to remember your adventures, you may feel overwhelmed. Second, your classmates will be younger than you are. That may not matter—you know yourself best. But if you are into sports, your age may make a difference. Some schools require you to stop competing when you become a certain age. Third, the cost of tuition increases every year and you may find that you are spending more for your education than you planned. On the other hand, you may be able to earn money during the year.

There are pros and cons. Evidence has shown that students who take a gap year often bring more to their college experiences and derive more from them as well. They spend the gap year productively, discover where their interests and talents lie, and with renewed maturity, they can focus on something they love.

If you have carefully considered the pros and cons, and you still want to take a year off between high school and college, do some research and get advice. Then plan. Careful planning is the key to the rewards you'll get. Start by visiting the Council on Standards for International Educational Travel website (http://www.csiet.org) for a list of reputable international programs and providers. CSIET's mission is to identify reputable international youth exchange programs and to provide leadership and support to the exchange and educational communities so that youth are provided with meaningful and safe international exchange experiences. You may also want to look at the "time out" programs included in Table 2.

Academic Programs

Choosing an academic program requires students to look closely at their planned 4-year high school program and their own strengths and weaknesses. As stated earlier, students who choose to accelerate by taking an out-of-school course may find themselves in the unenviable position of repeating that course in school at a much slower pace because the high school will not acknowledge the student's acceleration and mastery. Before you enroll in an academic course for which you want school credit and/or advanced placement, make sure that your school will cooperate. If you take an Advanced Placement course in a summer program, make sure that you take the AP test and that your score is recorded on your transcript. If you did not take the AP test, investigate taking the test when your school gives it. Enrichment courses like ancient Greek or Existentialism do not cause problems with schools because there is no expectation of school credit. Teenagers take enrichment courses

Table 2
Gap Year Programs

Gapyear
http://www.gapyear.com
This site features a wide variety of travel and planning ideas and offers resources for further reading.

Taking Off
http://www.takingoff.net
Taking Off describes itself as a service for individuals considering a gap year or any length of time away from your current situation. It offers a process that helps to clarify interests, define goals, identify options, and implement a safe, meaningful, and well-thought-out plan. Academic year and summer programs in North America, Europe, the Caribbean, Africa, Mexico, Central and South America, Europe, Asia, Israel, Australia, New Zealand, and the Pacific are open to high school juniors and seniors and college students.

The Center for Interim Programs
http://www.interimprograms.com
Founded in 1980, and with offices in New Jersey and Massachusetts, The Center for Interim Programs is a consulting service that can help you plan your gap year. The website offers sample programs and ideas.

The National Association for College Admission Counseling
http://www.nacacnet.org/studentinfo/articles/Pages/Gap-Year-.aspx
NACAC offers a wealth of information about gap years. They can provide referrals to accredited counselors. They suggest that you start by asking the following questions:

- » What do I want to learn?
- » How much structure do I want or need?
- » Where in the world do I want to be?
- » What kinds of things do I want to do?
- » What will I do when things get very difficult? What is my emergency plan?

College Express and **Admissions Quest**
http://www.collegexpress.com; http://www.admissionsquest.com
These websites provide a list of gap programs and websites to get you started.

Global Citizen Year
http://globalcitizenyear.org

Where There Be Dragons
http://www.wheretherebedragons.com

International Studies Abroad Inc. (ISA)
http://www.studiesabroad.com

Should I Take Time Off?
https://college.harvard.edu/admissions/preparing-college/should-i-take-time
Lastly, visit Harvard's website to read an interesting article titled *Time Out or Burn Out for the Next Generation.*

because they are interested in exploring a topic that is not normally taught in their middle or high school and are looking for a fast-paced, intense experience.

Learning style (i.e., the way you learn, including your preferred learning environment) should be a significant factor when choosing an academic course (Olszewski-Kubilius, 2007). Students who are highly organized, have strong study skills, and can work independently usually can handle an intensive accelerated course that moves quickly. Students who tend to be focused in one specific talent area may be more comfortable studying a single subject in great depth. The pace is slower, but no less intense. Some students do not have intellectual peers in their home school district and enroll in courses for social, as well as academic, reasons. These students may want to sample courses by taking one class in the morning and a different class in the afternoon. The courses may or may not appear on the student's transcript, so make sure that documentation is in your portfolio that eventually will go to the colleges to which you apply.

You'll want to keep several other considerations in mind as you choose an academic program, including:

- *Location*: If you are not accustomed to the part of the country where classes are located, ask the program director if you can speak with previous attendees. Preparing yourself for the weather in a different part of the country may seem trivial now, but inclement weather without proper clothing can be a real downer. You will also want to prepare yourself to navigate the area on your own by consulting maps (and travel guides if the program is overseas or in a big city, like New York City) and finding out information about public transportation in the area.
- *Class Size*: Are you comfortable in a lecture hall with 800 other students or do you need a small class? Check with the program director or previous attendees to find out the class size and if it is suitable to your learning preferences. If you are easily distracted, avoid the lecture hall or sit in the front row.

- *Recreation*: Do other teens bring bikes? What else might you need? Should teens leave electronic gadgets such as iPods at home? Most programs allow iPads and cell phones because they have multiple uses. However, it doesn't hurt to verify. Find out if the program offers additional outings on weekends and if there is an extra cost to participate in such outings.
- *Additional Qualifications*: Some programs require students to have previous experience or special qualifications. For example, some marine programs require students to have a valid SCUBA certification and strong swimming ability. Some require students to have strong research skills. Check with the program to see if any prerequisites are required, and if so, how you can go about arranging the completion of these requirements.
- *Staff to Student Ratio*: Check out the number of faculty or teachers per student, especially if you expect to be doing research. If there are 20 students per teacher, don't expect a lot of one-on-one mentoring. The ratio is particularly important if you are doing field research (e.g., an archaeology site) and recording scientific observations. Speak with previous attendees and ask what to expect.
- *Staff Qualifications*: Before you commit to a research program, verify the seriousness of the project. Are the leaders affiliated with a university or well-established research facility? Have the scientists published earlier work in the topic? Working with a research scientist in a laboratory is a remarkable opportunity, especially if you will be allowed to publish. The experience is likely to give you credibility when you apply to colleges. At the very least, it will give you some credentials in the field. Make sure you ask the researchers you work with for a letter of recommendation that can accompany your college application. If you wait until you are filling out applications, the researchers' memory of you may not be fresh.

Fine and Performing Arts

Fine and performing arts is a broad category that covers a multitude of talent areas including studio, performing, theater and visual arts, dance, music, and so forth. They all have at least one thing in common—because of school district budget cutbacks few young students are exposed to the arts through their schools. In many schools, all forms of the arts have quietly disappeared from school curricula. Until a few years ago, a school band was integral to elementary and middle schools. Students learned to read music while learning to play an instrument. Today, school art and music classes are no longer a given. School policymakers say that they had to choose between an arts teacher and a teacher who can teach science, math, social studies, or language arts. By implication, the arts have become something that children can do if their parents have the money to pay for it and if it's important to the family.

We live in a modern world where art and music are digitized, synthesized, and downloaded and it's easier to find a computer camp than a summer arts program. Some states (e.g., North and South Carolina) host year-round programs for students who can qualify. Summer programs are offered to middle and high school students. Some programs are free and others are quite expensive. Some programs are part of a national system of Governor's Schools providing intensive high-quality experiences focusing on diverse areas of art or science. Many states offer a residential Governor's School program only to students who are between their junior and senior years. Some are open to any state or out-of-state resident who can pay the cost of the program. Specific criteria for selection of students differ, depending on the state. For more information, including a list of schools with contact information, visit the website for the National Conference for Governor's Schools at http://ncogs.org.

Many young students who take summer classes in the arts are experimenting. That's one of the joys of summer—you can try out different areas to see if you have talent, to see if you want to spend more time acquiring expertise, or just for the exposure. If that sounds like you, you may be able to find a suitable arts program in the enrichment programs listed in this book. If you are at a higher level of expertise, ask your teachers about summer programs. During the summer, many private teachers teach at well-known institutes such as Tanglewood in Massachusetts and have connections to a wide variety of resources. If you are interested in performing arts, check your local newspaper for auditions and casting calls.

Here are a few tips to guide your choices:

- *Program Placement*: Your selected program should match your level of experience and accomplishment. This is less of a problem if the program requires auditions.
- *Quality of Faculty/Teachers*: Does the program use its advanced students as summer teachers or will you be working with artists who are fine teachers?
- *Career Opportunities*: If you are an advanced student, will the program or faculty open some doors for you?

If you are a serious artist, there are a host of summer programs with some scholarships available. Many universities and colleges are known for their summer arts programs. For example, North Carolina, New York, Connecticut, Ohio, and Oregon all have schools with fine reputations. The California State Summer School for the Arts (CSSSA) offers a talented group of high school students intensive training from professionals in music, theatre, video and film, visual arts, dance, and creative writing. Admission is competitive. Because it is a summer program, directors can hire a variety of well-known teachers who return to their own schools during winter sessions. This is one of the advantages of attending a summer program. Students are able to study with a variety of teachers, each with his or her area of expertise, and gain a different perspective from each. Needless to say, studying with a variety of people shows college admission faculty that you are committed to the arts. Make sure you get letters of recommendation from everyone who can speak to your work, even if you are not yet ready to apply to colleges.

People who study intensively may find that they need to take an "incubation" break during the summer. Sometimes it's healthier to sit by a lake watching nothing in particular. For dancers, it's an opportunity to rest one's body. For visual and similar creative artists, a short break can be a catalyst for renewed energy and motivation.

Service Learning

Another option for summer involvement is service learning. Service learning has been defined in many ways, but the core of its definition lies in connecting experiential learning (learning by doing) with community service. Service learning is a teaching and learning strategy that integrates meaningful community service with instruction and reflection to enrich the learning experience, teach civic responsibility, and strengthen communities. Young people apply academic skills to solving real-world issues, linking established learning objectives with genuine needs. They lead the process, with adults as partners, applying critical thinking and problem-solving skills to concerns such as hunger, pollution, and diversity.

Service learning is different from volunteering or internships because of its structure and connection to academics. Groups are well organized and led by adults in the field. Students may earn community service hours, but if earning service hours is the primary goal, you might consider an activity that is less challenging, such as reading to senior citizens who have lost their sight. Benefits of service learning for students include increased academic skills in relevant subjects (e.g., grammar, math, computers); an enhanced sense of confidence, self-efficacy, perseverance, and responsibility; and new perspectives on political, interpersonal, or occupational relationships (Terry, 2000). Researchers suggest that students benefit from service learning because it provides them with challenging extended curricula that stimulate advanced critical thinking skills, higher level thinking processes, and problem-solving abilities.

Examples of service learning projects are available at the following websites:

- Generator School Network (https://gsn.nylc.org)

- National Youth Leadership Council (http://www.nylc.org)
- National Association of Student Councils (NASC; http://www.nasc.us)

Youth Leadership Programs

Leadership camps provide young people with memories that last a lifetime, but they also have a very practical and expanding role. These camp experiences provide teens with the opportunity to develop knowledge, skills, and attitudes associated with socially responsible leadership. Students say that program activities inspire, encourage, and develop leadership skills. If you are looking for a leadership program, look beyond the general language into "how" they do this. Do they just talk about the merits of developing leadership skills? Or do they say specifically what attendees can expect in the way of courses? As an example, look at Brown University's Leadership Institute at http://www.brown.edu/ce/pre-college/overview.php. The courses are clearly stated, as is the way Brown extends learning into the general community.

Statewide Leadership Experiences

Many states nominate students to attend state leadership programs through their Governor's Schools. The other well-known programs are Boys and Girls State and the Hugh O'Brien Youth Foundation (HOBY). Boys State and Girls State are summer leadership and citizenship programs sponsored by the American Legion and the American Legion Auxiliary for high school students between their junior and senior years. Boys and Girls State programs are held in each of the U.S. states (excluding Hawaii), usually on a college campus within that state. Typically, students are nominated by an American Legion post, which pays the student's tuition.

Thousands of high school students will attend HOBY (http://www.hoby.org) programs each year, including Community

Leadership Workshops (CLeW), U.S. State Leadership Seminars, and the World Leadership Congress. CLeW is a one-day introductory HOBY leadership session for high school freshmen. Leadership Seminars are designed for high school sophomores to recognize their leadership talents and apply them in becoming effective, ethical leaders in their home, schools, workplace, and community. The World Leadership Congress, the next level of leadership training, is a weeklong intensive educational program held every summer in Washington, DC.

The National Association of Secondary School Principals sponsors summer leadership camps in many states. They also publish *Leadership for Student Activities*, a monthly magazine for members of the National Association of Student Councils, the National Honor Society, and the National Junior Honor Society. Each month during the school year, *Leadership for Student Activities* focuses on a topic of interest to student leaders in middle and high school and their advisers.

The National Association of Student Councils promotes and provides leadership development opportunities to prepare and empower student leaders to serve their schools and communities. For specific information on leadership camps in your area, contact your state branch of this organization.

Volunteer Programs

Volunteer programs require that you provide services to help others without the intention of a monetary reward, complete tasks for which you receive minimal payment, or join programs in which you pay to participate in helping others. If you are volunteering outside the United States, you should plan on a significant expense. If you want to volunteer in your community, start by asking yourself, "What's in my backyard?" Some organizations won't take volunteers because they can't train them or because their insurance won't cover volunteers. But there are enough places that welcome volunteers, so keep asking if you are interested in a particular venue or career field. The people you help will appreciate your efforts.

Teens usually volunteer for several reasons: to fulfill community service obligations, because of a belief in a cause bigger than themselves, to gain credentials or experience in a specific field, to explore career options, or because nothing else has an appeal. To truly explore career goals, volunteers must plan on participating in a program for a considerable length of time so they can see all of the aspects and talk to a lot of people about educational choices or other areas. Be prepared to ask, "What did you do that you are very glad you did?" and "What did you do that you haven't needed?" There is so much variance among programs that, again, there are only a few considerations that cross programs.

When looking for volunteer programs, start by asking your school counselors and teachers. Then use the Internet to find community directories of programs that have been certified or accredited by an outside agency. Look for programs in your backyard like the American Red Cross, local hospitals, your city's Department of Parks and Recreation, senior citizen assisted living facilities, Big Brothers Big Sisters, or the YMCA. VolunteerMatch publishes a list of opportunities (http://www.volunteermatch.org).

Internships

An internship offers you an opportunity to test your interest in an area before you make a commitment to further study or career preparation. Some programs let you try out what it is like to work in a supervised position all day, day after day, in a particular field. The word *intern* often refers to a variety of activities in which a person receives firsthand experience in a field, usually for minimum or no pay, under the direct guidance and supervision of a professional. Finding a position takes time because the number of internships in any one firm or agency is very limited. You may be able to find an internship through your high school guidance department or city council. Contacting the trade association in your field of interest can lead to an internship, as well as a lot of contacts. There is usually a trade association for every field. *Imagine*, a student magazine published by the Center for Talented Youth at Johns Hopkins University (http://cty.jhu.edu/imagine), includes a column in every issue spotlighting a career. The column "Exploring Career Options" usually includes an interview with someone in the field, as well as information on the required education, the job outlook, salary range, and resources for more information. They also include some information on internships.

The areas of service learning, community service, internships, and volunteerism intersect one another at different junctions. When you are looking for this type of activity, especially on the Internet, be aware that the terms mean different things to different people. Be creative in your search when looking for these types of programs.

Now that you know a little about each of the types of programs available, you'll want to decide which interests you most and move on to the next step: finding and selecting the right program for you.

Chapter 4

But How Do I Find a Program?

Once you've considered what kind of program you might be interested in, it's time to start looking for opportunities. You'll want to make sure that you peruse the programs in this book, but also ask your guidance counselor, teachers, and friends for suggestions. Sometimes, little-known programs in your community offer fabulous experiences.

Finding and Choosing a Summer Program

This book offers more than 200 programs, selected from a much larger group, whose organizers said their programs meet the needs of college-bound youth. The program you choose should be a good match for your needs. For example, if you are not accustomed to hiking, a rugged trek in Mongolia probably is not the program for you. If you are afraid of snakes, you may want to avoid the Southeast Asian rainforest. Some consultants believe that there are no bad programs, just bad fits.

Finding appropriate programs depends on the usual things such as location and cost. Your family might want some input on your choice of activity, especially if they are helping to pay for a program or if they are going to transport you. If you find that you are interested in everything, look at your own strengths and interests. Is there any area where you want to learn more? The following questions might help in your evaluation (Berger, 2014; Ware, 1990):

- What are your academic and social strengths?
- What academic or social weaknesses might you have that can be addressed in a summer program?
- What *new* opportunities (academics, recreational and/or social) would benefit or better prepare you for the future? What do *you* want to do?
- If you are involved in an activity in school, is there a summer experience where you can learn more about that activity?
- What are the criteria for acceptance to a program you are considering? If you want something academic, you need to plan at least 6 months in advance. You may need to take the PSAT or some other test to be eligible to participate.
- Do you have any health issues? (If you are horribly allergic to bees or plants, you may want to choose a program that keeps you away from wildlife.)

Some other nonacademic questions your parents should ask:

- How is the food? Does the program provide for special diets?
- What type of social activities does the program provide?
- Where will the student get medical care, if necessary? If a student requires medication, who will dispense it? Is a physician on call or on site each date? What are the credentials of people who staff the infirmary? How far is the nearest

hospital? What type of insurance does the camp offer in case a camper gets hurt?

- If a program stresses "communing with nature," is it really a nature camp or is it a regular program with outside activities?
- Summer is a great time to "unplug," to get away from electronics for a while. If the cell phone is home, how do campers contact their families? Are students allowed to send e-mail messages and are there rules governing the use of e-mail? Be sure to ask the program if campers have access to electronic games, computers, and video devices.

When you start to research summer opportunities, the following areas are important for you and your family to keep in mind.

- *Length*: Programs vary from one to 10 weeks. Length affects the skill level that can be reached and the overall cost.
- *Age range*: Determine the age range of participants and the way they are grouped to know whether a camper will be with peers or will be one of the oldest or youngest members.
- *Requirements*: In some types of programs, especially in academics and music, the requirements for application can provide a clue to what one can expect. For example, a music program that requires a tape or audition may involve more difficult orchestral music than a program that takes anyone who has had one year of lessons.
- *Size*: The overall number of participants, as well as the size of activity or study groups, affects the atmosphere of a program and the kinds of activities that are possible.
- *Individual attention*: Closely related to size is the ratio of leaders or teachers to participants. The lower the ratio, the more individual attention one can expect.
- *Leadership*: There is not one ideal background of a leader or teacher. They include professionals, experienced volunteers, and teachers at all levels: college faculty, public and private school teachers, and undergraduate teaching assistants. The common qualities that make them appropriate

are experience in their field, experience and pleasure in working with young people, and the flexibility and desire to be in a summer program setting.

- *Depth of experience*: Ask the staff and previous participants for specific examples of the activities and the skill level they develop to judge whether the program is an appropriate match for your abilities and goals.
- *Credit or not-for-credit courses*: A program's approach to credit is an integral part of its philosophy. Programs that do not grant credit want to encourage students to pursue a topic at length without being concerned about grades. Credit-granting programs view grades as a normal part of an academic experience.
- *Facilities and equipment*: The quality of the facilities and the amount of equipment impact the level of involvement. One computer for every two participants allows more work time than one computer for five participants. This also applies to laboratory, art, drama, music, and sports equipment.
- *Schedule*: Does the participant want to have every minute scheduled, or does he or she prefer a more relaxed pace that includes unscheduled free time?
- *Recreation*: To what extent are athletics or other recreational activities such as arts or drama offered or required? Some organizations require an hour or two of individual or team sports daily. Others view activities as optional.
- *Social activities*: Most programs plan informal group activities for participants to get to know one another. A few programs leave this up to the students.
- *Safety*: In all programs, safety is of paramount importance. Ask about the training and qualifications of the instructors, the certifications or inspections the program has passed, and the provisions that are made for safety.

Directories

This book is an example of the many directories of summer programs that exist. Many of the talent search programs publish directories that list camps and programs. Typically, someone has culled websites and categorized them, so the tedious work has been done for you. Before you start searching, go to the website of your state gifted advocacy group or The American Camping Association (http://www.acacamps.org). You will also find a list at http://www.hoagiesgifted.org/organizations.htm. Many of these groups offer directories or lists of programs on their websites. They may not endorse the programs, but you may be able to contact the group and ask if anyone has direct experience with a program that interests you. Major search engines like Google and Yahoo also have directories of summer programs. Other resources for directories can be found in Table 3.

Independent Consultants

One of the safest and most efficient ways of finding a summer program is to use a private licensed independent consultant. These consultants often visit the programs while they are in session and can tell you what to expect. If you need help finding a consultant, contact the Independent Educational Consultants Association (http://www.iecaonline.com). IECA member consultants counsel students and their families in the selection of educational programs based on the student's individual needs and talents. The fee varies with the counselor's expertise and geographical area.

Many communities have camp advisors or summer enrichment fairs. Camp advisors frequently do not charge families; rather, they charge the programs to which they refer clients. This means that you may not hear about small programs that do not want to pay camp advisor fees. If you live in a community where there is a gifted advocacy group, find out if they publish a list of summer programs or sponsor a summer enrichment fair. Another excellent resource is the American Camping Association (http://www.acacamps.org). Its website offers a "Find a Camp" tool (http://find.acacamps.org).

Table 3
Resources and Directories for Summer Programs

National Association for Gifted Children (NAGC) Resource Directory
http://giftedandtalentedresourcesdirectory.com
Information on all types of resources. Entries subscribe to this service and supply the information.

Educational Opportunity Guide
Duke University Talent Identification Program (TIP)
https://eog.tip.duke.edu/
Duke TIP us a talent search program that publishes this guide of summer opportunities.

Educational Program Guide
Center for Talent Development
http://www.ctd.northwestern.edu/resources/educational-program-guide
The Center for Talent Development (CTD) offers a potpourri of summer programs for all ages.

***Imagine*: Opportunities and Resources**
Johns Hopkins University
http://cty.jhu.edu/imagine
Written for gifted students in grades 7–12, *Imagine* features career profiles, student-written articles about competitions and summer programs, advice for college planning, brain teasers, college reviews, student creative work, and more.

Institute for Educational Advancement (IEA)
http://www.educationaladvancement.org
IEA's Gifted Resource Center offers activities and information for gifted youngsters. The list includes contests, scholarships, a distance learning opportunities search engine, a searchable program database, school search, and testing and counseling resources.

Several other websites are available for searching out appropriate programs, including:

- Davidson Institute for Talent Development, which has an effective search engine to find camps or precollege programs (http://www.davidsongifted.org/db/browse_resources_218.aspx);
- Camp Page, which provides links to accredited U.S. and Canadian summer camps and jobs (http://www.camppage.com); and
- Teen Ink, whose list (http://teenink.com/Summer) runs the gamut from short-term work-related jobs, to writing

and engineering camps, to those located on university campuses, ships, and overseas.

Some summer opportunities are designed to attract bright teens to a career field. For example, Virginia Space Coast Scholars, at NASA Wallops Flight Facility on Wallops Island, VA, selects students for a weeklong program based on their scientific interests and motivation to learn about NASA's opportunities. The students engage in an online STEM learning experience and can qualify for a weeklong residential summer academy.

If you have special needs, contact your advocacy group and ask about camps. For example, Camp AZDA is one of many camps across the U.S. that is designed for kids with diabetes and run by the American Diabetes Association (http://www.diabetes.org/in-my-community/diabetes-camp/camps/azda.html).

Paying for Programs

Before selecting and applying to a summer program, discuss the costs of summer programs with your parents or guardians. Ask your parents for a budget of how much money they are willing and able to spend on a summer program. Make sure that when you look for programs, you don't discount programs with little or no fees attached. Sometimes, the best summer programs are those run by your local university or parks department for a minimal fee. Sometimes, summer opportunities can be as simple as volunteering at your local church, school, hospital, museum, or zoo, or working as an unpaid intern in your county or city offices. In this case, you'll only need to set aside enough money for your transportation to and from your position. Assuming that you have already looked at no-cost programs, the first and most obvious strategy is to ask the program you want to attend for a scholarship. Some programs have scholarship money set aside for students who cannot afford the program.

There are two types of financial aid: merit-based and need-based. Merit-based funds are very competitive but always worth trying for. The Davidson Institute (http://www.davidsonfellows.org) has resources for merit-based aid, as does the Jack Kent Cooke Foundation (http://www.jkcf.org), which is gaining a reputation as a good source for need-based aid, particularly for undergraduate programs. Need-based funds are usually based on your family income and generally require that your family submit their most recent tax statement. Check the American Camp Association website (http://www.acacamps.org) for information on some need-based programs. For example, one such program is the University of Virginia (UVA) Summer Language Institute, which offers some need-based scholarships.

You should contact your state gifted association and local parent groups, which often have merit-based and need-based funds set aside to help gifted or talented children and teens attend summer programs. State gifted associations are listed on the National Association for Gifted Children website (http://www.nagc.org). Another option is to check with your school's PTA or PTO, and local organizations like the American Legion, Junior League, religious groups, or other volunteer fraternal and sororal organizations. Such community groups set aside money to help students in need. By contacting these organizations, you may find opportunities for scholarships or help for minor expenses like equipment, travel, or books. If you are persuasive, you may even be able to convince a local business to pay for a summer program in exchange for work during the winter or some other commodity. Check with your local Chamber of Commerce for information.

If you can't find money donated by local or state organizations or businesses, don't fret. You can always organize your own fund-raising possibilities by asking neighbors if you can do yard or housework for them in exchange for a donation. Garage sales, bake sales, and car washes are all effective ways for several students to pitch in to help raise money for summer programs that will be split among the group. Babysitting for friends and family, providing care for elderly family members, designing websites, or even taking on a part-time job on the weekends during the school year and up to the point when you leave for your summer program are all viable options of raising the money you plan to spend during your summer program.

The more care you take in seeking the answers to large and small questions, the greater probability of success in finding an appropriate and valuable summer pursuit. Whatever you decide to do, have a great summer!

References

American Camp Association. (2005). *Directions: Youth development outcomes of the camp experience.* Retrieved from http://www.acacamps.org/research/marsh/mtreviewlit.php

AP Capstone™. (2015). Retrieved from https://lp.collegeboard.org/ap-capstone

Berger, S. (2014). *College planning for gifted students: Choosing and getting into the right college.* Waco, TX: Prufrock Press.

Davidson, J., & Davidson, B. (2004). *Genius denied: How to stop wasting our brightest young minds.* NY: Simon & Schuster.

Ellis, D. (2014). *Becoming a master student* (14th ed.). Stamford, CT: Cengage Learning. Retrieved from http://www.daveellisleadership.com

Marine careers. (2014). Retrieved from http://www.whoi.edu/main/marine-careers

McClarty, K. L. (2015). Life in the fast lane: Effects of early grade acceleration on high school and college outcomes. *Gifted Child Quarterly, 59(1)*, 3–13.

Moshan, M., Mendelsohn, D., & Shapiro, M. (2006). *Rock the SAT.* Columbus, OH: McGraw-Hill.

Olszewski-Kubilius, P. (2007). The role of summer programs in developing the talents of gifted students. In J. L. VanTassel-Baska (Ed.), *Serving gifted learners beyond the traditional classroom* (pp. 13–32). Waco, TX: Prufrock Press.

Terry, A.W. (2000). An early glimpse: Service learning from an adolescent perspective. *Journal of Secondary Gifted Education, 11*, 115–135.

Ware, C. (1990). *Discovering interests and talents through summer experiences.* Retrieved from http://www.ericdigests.org/pre-9216/talents.htm (ED321496)

What is TASP? (n.d.). Retrieved from http://www.telluride association.org/programs/high_school_students/tasp/tasp_general_info.html

What Yale looks for. (n.d.) Retrieved from http://admissions.yale.edu/what-yale-looks-for

Part II

Summer Program Directory

Auburn University Summer Science Institute

Contact: Mary Lou Ewald, Director, Science and Math Outreach

Address: COSAM Outreach
131 Sciences Center Classroom Building
Auburn University, AL 36849

Phone: 334-844-5745

Fax: 334-844-5740

E-mail: ewaldml@auburn.edu

Website: http://www.auburn.edu/cosam/departments/outreach/programs/SSI/index.htm

Program Type: Academic Enrichment

Grade/Age Levels: Rising grades 11–12

Description: The Auburn University Summer Science Institute (AU-SSI) is an annual weeklong summer residential science program for high-achieving students with an aptitude and interest in the fields of science and math. The program, supported by the College of Sciences and Mathematics at Auburn University, partners students with experienced AU Science and Math research faculty to explore topics more advanced than what is typically taught in a public or private high school environment. Applicants must reside in Alabama or Georgia. Seating is limited to 24 and will be granted on an academically competitive basis.

AU-SSI is offered at no cost to its participants. Selected participants may attend regardless of their financial status. All educational and recreational programming, meals, and lodging are provided free of charge to the participants. AU-SSI is not a science camp. It is an institute for highly motivated

Description, Continued high school juniors and seniors with a serious interest in pursuing a math, science, or related degree. Acceptance into the program is an excellent addition to an ambitious high school student's résumé.

Sample topics include: Quantum Electrodynamics, Geologic Isotope Dating, Mathematics of Music on Compact Discs, Scanning Electron and Digital Microscopy, DNA Sequencing and Bioinformatics, and Field Biology experiences.

ALABAMA

The BEST Experience
Be an Engineering Student Experience

Contact: Jacob Kerstiens, Coordinator

Address: The University of Alabama in Huntsville
College of Engineering
EB 157
Huntsville, AL 35899

Phone: 256-824-6877

Fax: 256-824-7412

E-mail: jacob.kerstiens@uah.edu

Website: http://www.uah.edu/eng/outreach/summer-camp

Program Type: Math, Sciences, Engineering, and Computer Science/Technology

Grade/Age Levels: Rising grades 11–12

Description: The BEST Experience is a weeklong residential program that gives high school students a taste of what being an engineering student at UAH is all about. Students will go to engineering classes, perform hands-on experiments in engineering labs, participate in UAH student life activities, work on project teams, live in the residence halls, and eat at campus dining facilities.

Astronomy Camp for Teens

Contact: Dr. Donald McCarthy, Jr., Astronomer, Camp Director

Address: Steward Observatory
The University of Arizona
933 N. Cherry Ave.
Tucson, AZ 85721

Phone: 520-621-4079

Fax: 520-621-9843

E-mail: dmccarthy@as.arizona.edu

Website: http://www.astronomycamp.org

Program Type: Math, Sciences, Engineering, and Computer Science/Technology

Grade/Age Levels: Ages 13–19

Description: Astronomy Camps are immersion adventures in doing science. Participants become astronomers operating large telescopes (12, 20, 40, 60, 61-inch diameters), interacting with leading scientists, and interpreting their own scientific observations. The camps are held in the "Sky Island" environment of Mt. Lemmon SkyCenter (9,200 feet). Daytime activities include solar observing, construction projects, interactive talks, inquiry-based activities led by astronomers and educators, and tours of the UA Mirror Lab and other facilities.

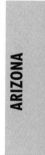

Honors Summer Academy

Address: Honors Summer Academy
1027 E 2nd St, Box 210006
Tucson, AZ, 85721

Phone: 520-621-6901

Fax: 520-621-8655

E-mail: honorsacademy@email.arizona.edu

Website: http://www.honors.arizona.edu/summeracademy

Program Type: Academic Enrichment

Grade/Age Levels: Rising grade 12 and up

Description: The University of Arizona Honors College's Honors Summer Academy is a program for high-ability and high-achieving high school students who have completed their junior or senior year. The Honors Summer Academy provides students with the ability to take UA Honors College courses taught by Honors Faculty members. These interdisciplinary courses include work in the humanities, social sciences, and science. Students also have the opportunity to live in a residence hall, participate in off-campus classes and field trips, and have structured study time.

Alexa Café

Address: iD Tech Camps
910 E. Hamilton Ave., Ste. 300
Campbell, CA 95008

Phone: 1-408-709-8324

Fax: 1-408-871-2228

E-mail: info@idtech.com

Website: http://www.alexacafe.com

Program Type: Math, Sciences, Engineering, and Computer Science/Technology

Grade/Age Levels: Ages 10–15

Description: This summer, uncover a hidden talent. Meet new friends. Make a difference. At Alexa Café, girls ages 10–15 collaborate around café tables and can learn to code apps, produce films, design websites, develop wearable electronics, and more. High-energy, hands-on courses are taught in small clusters of just eight girls per instructor, uniquely emphasizing leadership, philanthropy, brand identity, and innovation. Plus, like other iD Tech summer programs, Alexa Café is inclusive of every background, skill level, and learning style.

Alexa Café has expanded to prestigious campuses nationwide, including Mills College, Bryn Mawr, Georgia Tech, and others. Now it's the largest all-girls tech camp in the country. Courses include Sugar Coded, Electric Latte, Game Swirl, Design Barista, Cinema Twist, Javaccino, Café Electric, Game Pop, and Cinemocha. No matter your passion, technology should be fun and meaningful. Join the Girls in Tech movement today!

In addition to Alexa Café, iD Tech also offers coed summer programs for ages 7–17, half-day camps for aspiring innovators ages 6–9, and 2-week, overnight academies for teens ages 13–18.

Asian American Journalists Association (AAJA) JCamp

Contact:	Justin Seiter, Program Associate
Address:	JCamp Asian American Journalists Association 5 Third St., Ste. 1108 San Francisco, CA 94103
Phone:	415-346-2051
Fax:	415-346-6343
E-mail:	justins@aaja.org
Website:	http://www.aaja.org
Program Type:	Academic Enrichment
Grade/Age Levels:	Grades 9–11
Description:	JCamp is a multicultural journalism program for talented high school students. This all expenses-paid camp brings together 42 students from diverse backgrounds across the nation for 6 days of intensive journalism training by professional mentors and high-profile industry speakers.

California College of the Arts Pre-College Program

Address: California College of the Arts
5212 Broadway
Oakland, CA 94618-1426

Phone: 510-594-3638

E-mail: precollege@cca.edu

Website: http://www.cca.edu/academics/precollege

Program Type: Fine, Performing, and Visual Arts; Academic Enrichment

Grade/Age Levels: Grades 6–12

Description: The Pre-College Program at California College of the Arts provides an opportunity for high school students to study art, architecture, design, or creative writing in an art school setting while earning three college credits. The program also enables participants to develop strong portfolio pieces for college admissions. Scholarships are available.

California Polytechnic University Architecture Summer Career Workshop

Contact: Dr. Mark Cabrinha, Associate Professor, Workshop Director

Address: Architecture Summer Career Workshop
California Polytechnic University,
San Luis Obispo
Architecture Department/
College of Continuing Education
San Luis Obispo, CA 93407

Phone: 805-756-2855

E-mail: mcabrinh@calpoly.edu

Website: http://architecture.calpoly.edu/about/summer-career

Program Type: Academic Enrichment

Grade/Age Levels: Grades 10–11

Description: The Architecture Department will offer an intensive 4-week in-residence workshop designed for high school students considering architecture as a career or developing a design portfolio. Students are presented an in-depth view of the career through hands-on experience in studio design exercises, lectures, projects, and field trips. Activities cover architectural design and history, computer applications, building science, structural engineering, and site planning. Studios and lectures are taught by the faculty of the College of Architecture and Environmental Design. Education and career advising are integral elements of the program.

California State Summer School for the Arts

Address: California State School for the Arts
P.O. Box 1077
Sacramento, CA 95812-1077

Phone: 916-229-5160

Fax: 916-229-5170

E-mail: application@csssa.org

Website: http://www.ccsssa.org

Program Type: Fine, Performing, and Visual Arts

Grade/Age Levels: Grades 9–12

Description: For 4 weeks each July and August, a talented group of high school students receive intensive training from professionals in music, theatre, video and film, visual arts, dance, creative writing, and animation on the campus of California Institute of the Arts in Valencia. Camp has a competitive application process with a deadline of February 28. Financial aid is available.

Camp Ocean Pines

Contact: Chris Cameron, Executive Director

Address: Camp Ocean Pines
1473 Randall Drive
Cambria, CA 93428

Phone: 805-927-0254

Fax: 805-927-2610

E-mail: admin@campoceanpines.org

Website: http://www.campoceanpines.org

Program Type: Academic Enrichment

Grade/Age Levels: Ages 7–18

Description: These overnight 6–8 day camps for ages 7–15 provide specialty activities for students to choose from including target sports (such as archery and tomahawk throwing), primitive skills (such as fire building and animal tracking), arts and crafts, and off-site trips. Camp Ocean Pines also offers programs especially for teens ages 14–18, the Hawaiian Adventure Trip, the Great California Road Trip, and the Counselor in Training Program.

Digital Media Academy

Address: Digital Media Academy
718 University Ave. Ste 100
Los Gatos, CA 95032

Phone: 866-656-3342

E-mail: info@digitalmediaacademy.org

Website: https://www.digitalmediaacademy.org

Program Type: Math, Sciences, Engineering, and Computer Science/Technology; Fine, Performing, and Visual Arts

Grade/Age Levels: Ages 9–19

Description: At Digital Media Academy, students learn by doing with hands-on instruction from industry professionals who have real-world experience. DMA builds and strengthens STEM (Science, Technology, Engineering & Math) skills. DMA alumni include television and music producers, filmmakers and professional photographers, as well as game and app developers. Camps are offered at universities across the U.S. and Canada, including Stanford University, the University of Texas at Austin, Northwestern University, New York University, George Washington University, the University of Toronto, and more.

Economics for Leaders (EFL)

Address: Economics for Leaders
Foundation for Teaching Economics (FTE)
260 Russell Blvd., Ste. B
Davis, CA 95616-3839

Phone: 530-757-4630

Fax: 530-757-4636

E-mail: information@fte.org

Website: http://www.fte.org/student-programs/economics-for-leaders-program

Program Type: Academic Enrichment; Leadership/Service/Volunteer

Grade/Age Levels: Rising grades 11–12

Description: This one-week program on economics and leadership has programs at various sites across the U.S. The Economics for Leaders programs are open to students completing their junior year in high school. These leadership retreats are held on prestigious college campuses throughout the United States and combine leadership and economics instruction. Economics professors and nationally recognized leadership facilitators lead in-depth discussions and activities designed to teach participants to understand and appreciate different leadership styles, develop insight into economic behavior, and foster an economic way of thinking about public policy choices. FTE bases the EFL curriculum on experiential learning, with activities, lessons, and discussions held in both indoor and outdoor settings.

Idyllwild Arts Summer Program

Contact: Ms. Diane Dennis, Registrar

Address: Idyllwild Arts
Box 38, 52500 Temecula Rd.
Idyllwild, CA 92549

Phone: 951-659-2171 ext. 2365

Fax: 951-655-4552

E-mail: summer@idyllwildarts.org

Website: http://www.idyllwildarts.org

Program Type: Fine, Performing, and Visual Arts

Grade/Age Levels: Ages 5–18

Description: Since 1950, the Idyllwild Arts Summer Program has offered intensive workshops in dance, film-video, music, theatre, visual arts, and creative writing to students of all ages and abilities, including families.

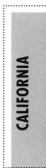

iD Tech Camps

Address: iD Tech Camps
910 E. Hamilton Ave., Ste. 300
Campbell, CA 95008

Phone: 1-408-709-8324

Fax: 1-408-871-2228

E-mail: info@idtech.com

Website: http://www.idtech.com

Program Type: Math, Sciences, Engineering, and Computer Science/Technology

Grade/Age Levels: Ages 7–17

Description: Code, game, create! At iD Tech Camps, students ages 7–17 design video games, mod Minecraft, code apps, engineer robots, build websites, produce films, and more. Hands-on learning takes place in small clusters of just eight students per instructor, guaranteed. Campers make friends and learn 21st-century skills that give them a competitive advantage for school and future STEM careers. These weeklong, day, and overnight programs are held at prestigious campuses nationwide, including Stanford, Princeton, Caltech, Yale, Rice, and more. Diverse courses are inclusive of every gender, background, skill level, and learning style.

In addition to iD Tech Camps, the company also offers all-girls programs for ages 10–15, half-day camps for aspiring innovators ages 6–9, and 2-week, overnight academies for teens ages 13–18. Visit http://www.idtech.com or call 1-888-709-8324 to find the right program for you.

iD Game Design & Development Academy

Address: iD Tech Camps
910 E. Hamilton Ave., Ste. 300
Campbell, CA 95008

Phone: 1-408-709-8324

Fax: 1-408-871-2228

E-mail: info@idtech.com

Website: http://www.idgamedevacademy.com

Program Type: Math, Sciences, Engineering, and Computer Science/Technology

Grade/Age Levels: Ages 13–18

Description: Game world meets real world at the iD Game Design & Development Academy, where teens ages 13–18 gain a competitive edge for college and future STEM careers. At this 2-week, precollege summer academy, students design video games, develop apps for iPhone and Android, model 3D characters, mod Minecraft, and more. Get fully immersed in technology by competing in gaming tournaments, touring a game design studio, creating a cutting-edge college portfolio, and interacting with industry pros. These summer academies are held at prestigious universities nationwide, including Harvard, Stanford, Villanova, Emory, and others.

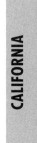

iD Programming Academy

Address: iD Tech Camps
910 E. Hamilton Ave., Ste. 300
Campbell, CA 95008

Phone: 1-408-709-8324

Fax: 1-408-871-2228

E-mail: info@idtech.com

Website: http://www.idprogrammingacademy.com

Program Type: Math, Sciences, Engineering, and Computer Science/Technology

Grade/Age Levels: Ages 13–18

Description: Calling all teen coders! At iD Programming Academy, teens ages 13–18 get immersed in technology. Students program with C++ and Java, code apps, mod Minecraft, engineer robots, program websites with HTML and PHP, and more. Teens tour a development studio, create a cutting-edge college portfolio, meet new friends, and interact with industry pros. These 2-week, precollege summer academies are held at prestigious universities nationwide, including Stanford, UCLA, Yale, Princeton, NYU, and others. There's no better way to gain a competitive advantage for college and future STEM careers.

Ignite LA Student Science Awards

Address: Earthwatch
114 Western Ave.
Boston, MA 02134

Phone: 1-800-776-0188

Fax: 978-450-1200

E-mail: fellowshipawards@earthwatch.org

Website: http://earthwatch.org/education/student-fellowships/ignite

Program Type: Internships/Paid Positions

Grade/Age Levels: Ages 15–18

Description: Earthwatch's Ignite LA Student Science Awards offers Los Angeles County high school students, ages 15–18, an opportunity to spend 2 weeks during the summer at a scientific research station, where students will conduct a variety of field and laboratory research activities focused on the world's most pressing environmental challenges. The aim is to excite the students' imagination, expand their potential, and stimulate their curiosity about science and technology. Ignite is a competitive fellowship program that rewards creative thinkers and risk takers. The program is funded by an outside donor and implemented by Earthwatch. This program does not require prior experience helping a scientist conduct research. Students are assigned to sites selected by Earthwatch for the quality of research and educational commitment of the scientific staff. For more information, please visit the website.

Institute for Educational Advancement Apprenticeship Program

Contact: Apprenticeship Program Coordinator

Address: Institute for Educational
Advancement – Apprenticeship
569 S. Marengo Ave.
Pasadena, CA 91101

Phone: 626-403-8900

Fax: 626-403-8905

E-mail: apprenticeship@educationaladvancement.org

Website: http://www.educationaladvancement.org

Program Type: Academic Enrichment

Grade/Age Levels: Grades 9–11

Description: Through its Apprenticeship Program, the Institute for Educational Advancement (IEA) links gifted students with mentors who advance each participant's skills through the application of knowledge and exposure to real-world experiences. These life lessons in personal and intellectual development are invaluable to their growth and assist them in making pertinent connections for the future.

Available apprenticeships vary by year. Apprenticeships take place in the Los Angeles area, with occasional satellite sites, and typically last 3 to 7 weeks. Past apprenticeships have included industrial design, medical research, architecture, biomathematics, biology, law, business, astronomy, communications, physics, and neuroscience.

Marine Technology Society Summer Internship Program for High School Students

Address: Marine Technology Society
P.O. Box 371348
San Diego, CA 92137-1348

Phone: 410-884-5330

Fax: 410-884-9060

E-mail: studentaffairs@mts-sandiego.com

Website: http://www.mts-sandiego.org

Program Type: Math, Sciences, Engineering, and Computer Science/Technology

Grade/Age Levels: Grades 11–12

Description: The San Diego Section of the Marine Technology Society has a summer internship program for high school students interested in the ocean professions. The San Diego MTS Program is a 6-week summer experience for motivated high school students hosted by one of MTS' corporate sponsors. Students get hands-on science and technology experiences, while building important scientific, technical, and employment skills under the direction of a workplace mentor. Students also receive a $2,160 stipend upon successful completion of the program.

QuestBridge College Prep Scholarship

Address: 115 Everett Avenue
Palo Alto, CA 94301

Phone: 650-331-3280; 888-275-2054

Fax: 650-653-2516

E-mail: questions@questbridge.org

Website: http://www.questbridge.org

Program Type: Academic Enrichment

Grade/Age Levels: Grade 11

Description: The QuestBridge College Prep Scholarship prepares outstanding low-income high school juniors to become successful applicants to leading colleges. Awards include full scholarships to college summer programs at Brandeis, Harvard, Emory, Notre Dame, Stanford, and Yale; personalized one-on-one college admissions counseling; invitations to QuestBridge National College Admissions Conferences held on college campuses around the country; and more. Students who apply for the College Prep Scholarship have a head start on the QuestBridge National College Match, a program that pairs high-achieving, low-income high school seniors with admission and full 4-year scholarships to 35 QuestBridge partner colleges, including Amherst College, Pomona College, Princeton University, Rice University, Stanford University, Williams College, and Yale University.

The Salk High School Scholars Program

Contact: Dona Mapston, Education Outreach

Address: 10010 N. Torrey Pines Rd.
La Jolla, CA 92037

Phone: 858-453-4100

Fax: 858-550-9960

E-mail: mapston@salk.edu

Website: http://www.salk.edu/about/education_outreach.html

Program Type: Internships/Paid Positions

Grade/Age Levels: Ages 16–18

Description: Students from throughout the San Diego area gather at the Salk Institute every summer to participate in hands-on laboratory experiences under the mentorship of a Salk scientist. Founded more than 30 years ago, the program helps fulfill Dr. Jonas Salk's vision of providing opportunities for local high school students to experience life in a scientific laboratory, and explore the possibility of a career in science. Throughout the 8-week program, which includes one nonpaid training week and a 7-week paid internship, students are involved with a full-time research project as well as enrichment activities. Students learn how to formulate and test hypotheses, prepare experiments, and draw conclusion from data. They also learn to maintain laboratory notebooks and take part in regular lab meetings and group discussions. At the end of the program, students present their research projects to their mentors, lab members, and families.

Applicants must be San Diego county residents and be able to commit to 40 hours a week for the duration of the program.

Santa Clara University Summer Engineering Seminar (SES)

Contact: Shane Wibeto, SES Coordinator

Address: Santa Clara University
School of Engineering
500 El Camino Real
Santa Clara, CA 95053-4728

Phone: 408-554-4728

E-mail: summerengineeringseminar@scu.edu

Website: http://scu.edu/engineering/about/ses.cfm

Program Type: Math, Sciences, Engineering, and Computer Science/Technology

Grade/Age Levels: Grades 10–11

Description: The SES is a special summer experience for high school students who may be curious about engineering. The program is designed to acquaint high school students with the engineering profession, the academic expectations of college, and university life. It provides participants with a chance to explore the possibilities of engineering as a career while living in a university residence hall. Participants take specially designed introductory workshops taught by engineering faculty that span many disciplines of the field of engineering. Workshops are a mix of interactive lectures and interactive activities and labs. If accepted, this program has no cost to participants outside of transportation to and from the university. Women and other underrepresented groups in the field of engineering are highly encouraged to apply. Priority will be given to applicants who lack the means to access engineering courses, programs, and activities.

Stanford Pre-Collegiate Summer Institutes

Contact: Diana Sunshine

Address: Stanford Pre-Collegiate Studies
Stanford University
220 Panama Street
Stanford, CA 94305

Phone: 800-372-3749 (option 3) or 650-721-9325

Fax: 866-835-3312 or 650-721-9383

E-mail: summerinstitutes@stanford.edu

Website: http://summerinstitutes.stanford.edu

Program Type: Academic Enrichment

Grade/Age Levels: Grades 6–11

Description: The Summer Institutes are 2–4-week residential programs for academically talented and motivated middle and high school students. The Summer Institutes provide an opportunity for these students to pursue their intellectual curiosity and meet others who share their interests and abilities.

Summer Institutes participants live in supervised Stanford housing and are taught by Stanford instructors. Students engage in intensive study in a single course, and they are introduced to topics not typically presented at their grade level, including arts and humanities, business, computer science, engineering, legal studies, mathematics, social science, physical and biological science, and writing. The instructors are assisted by undergraduate and graduate student mentors who have expertise in the course subject areas. These mentors serve a dual role of Residential Counselor and Teaching Assistant so that the academic and social aspects of the program are tightly integrated.

The Summer Institutes provide a taste of college life in the beautiful surroundings of the Stanford campus.

Stanford Summer Humanities Institute

Contact: Diana Sunshine

Address: Stanford University
220 Panama Street
Stanford, CA 94305

Phone: 888-423-6040 or 650-721-2947

Fax: 866-835-3312 or 650-721-9383

E-mail: summerhumanities@stanford.edu

Website: http://summerhumanities.stanford.edu

Program Type: Academic Enrichment

Grade/Age Levels: Grades 10–11

Description: Led by Stanford professors, the Summer Humanities Institute lets rising high school juniors and seniors explore the big questions at the heart of the humanities: how and when can big ideas transform society? When is the use of force legitimate? How can we define the limits of individual rights?

Students live in residence for 3 weeks on the beautiful Stanford campus. They spend the first 2 weeks intensively studying and researching a topic in the humanities, attending daily lectures by the faculty members, and participating in group discussions and activities in the afternoon. There is also downtime for extracurricular fun, as well as supervised off-campus excursions to places of cultural and natural interest around the Bay Area.

During the third week, students work closely with their professors, graduate students, and writing mentors to produce original research projects. These papers present an opportunity for students to use what they have learned at Stanford to develop their own answers to the central questions that are

Description, Continued addressed by the humanities. Students are introduced to research methods, as well as to library and online resources. And they'll have something very impressive to show for it!

Stanford Youth Orchestra

Contact: Diana Sunshine

Address: Stanford University
220 Panama Street
Stanford, CA 94305

Phone: 888-423-6040 or 650-721-2947

Fax: 866-835-3312 or 650-721-9383

E-mail: youthorchestra@stanford.edu

Website: http://youthorchestra.stanford.edu

Program Type: Academic Enrichment; Fine, Performing and Visual Arts

Grade/Age Levels: Grades 8–11

Description: The Stanford Youth Orchestra brings the finest young musicians from around the world to participate in a 3-week intensive orchestral and academic program on the beautiful campus of Stanford University. Bringing together world-renowned faculty instructors, the Stanford Youth Orchestra provides participants with exceptional orchestral training in the state-of-the-art Bing Concert Hall, and within Stanford's peerless intellectual and interdisciplinary environment.

In addition to orchestral studies, practice, and performance, participants also attend a range of workshops that bring together music, science, technology, and culture. These workshops are led by Stanford faculty from the Department of Music as well as the Center for Computer Research in Music and Acoustics (CCRMA).

During their stay at Stanford, SYO participants are closely mentored by members of the Stanford Symphony Orchestra and supervised by residential counselors, who serve dual roles as camp counselor and teaching assistant. Whether participants have an interest

Description, Continued in majoring in music in college, or in maintaining a serious engagement with music while majoring in other subjects, SYO mentors will serve as role models to participants both musically and academically.

Stanford University Mathematics Camp (SUMaC)

CALIFORNIA

Contact: Diana Sunshine

Address: Stanford University
220 Panama Street
Stanford, CA 94305

Phone: 888-423-6040 or 650-721-2947

Fax: 866-835-3312 or 650-721-9383

E-mail: sumacinfo@stanford.edu

Website: http://sumac.stanford.edu

Program Type: Academic Enrichment

Grade/Age Levels: Grades 11–12

Description: SUMaC is designed for high school students who have exceptional interest and ability in mathematics and seek to be challenged in mathematics. Students live in supervised Stanford housing during the 4 weeks of intensive, in-depth mathematical pursuits.

The program engages students by introducing the course material through problems that are of historical significance, that are important to the development of mathematics, that have applications to current lines of research in mathematics and the sciences, and that will be found interesting by students who enjoy mathematics.

SUMaC provides an environment that fosters social and intellectual development centered on the study and enjoyment of mathematics.

Stanford Medical Youth Science Program (SMYSP)

Contact: Dr. Judith Ned, Executive Director

Address: Stanford Medical Youth Science Program
Stanford University
Stanford Prevention Research Center/MSOB
1265 Welch Road, Room X324
Stanford, CA 94305-5705

Phone: 650-498-4514

Fax: 650-725-6247

E-mail: youth.science@stanford.edu

Website: http://smysp.stanford.edu

Program Type: Math, Sciences, Engineering, and Computer Science/Technology

Grade/Age Levels: Grades 10–11

Description: The Stanford Medical Youth Science Program (SMYSP) offers university and school-based programs for low-income and underrepresented minority high school students. The hallmark is the 5-week Summer Residential Program held on Stanford's campus for students interested in science, medicine, and public health. Low-income students from any ethnic background are welcome to apply. SMYSP selects 24 high school students who live and attend schools in Northern and Central California. Ten Stanford University undergraduate students direct the Summer Residential Program and serve as counselors and mentors. The student counselors live with the high school students in a residential house on the Stanford University campus 7 days a week, including weekends. Please note that SMYSP is not a program for gifted students.

CALIFORNIA

Summer of Art College Prep Program

Address: Summer of Art College Prep Program
Otis College of Art and Design
9045 Lincoln Blvd.
Los Angeles, CA 90045

Phone: 310-665-6864; 800-527-6847

Fax: 310-665-6854

E-mail: soa@otis.edu

Website: http://www.otis.edu/soa

Program Type: Fine, Performing, and Visual Arts

Grade/Age Levels: Ages 15 and up

Description: Summer of Art is an intensive, 4-week, pre-college program for individuals 15 and older who wish to study at one of the top art and design colleges in the country. Serious young artists seeking to strengthen and enhance their art and design skills, as well as students with limited art training, are invited to participate. Courses may include Architecture/Landscape/Interiors, 2D Animation, Digital Media: Concept Development and Creativity, Observational Drawing, Fashion Design, Graphic Design, Illustration, Life Drawing, Painting, Photography, Printmaking and Urban Art, Product Design, and Toy Design. English language immersion courses for English language learners are offered. Students can earn college credit for completing the courses. Housing is available.

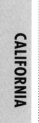

University of California–Davis Young Scholars Program

Contact: Dr. Rick Pomeroy, Program Director

Address: University of California
School of Education
One Shields Ave.
Davis, CA 95616-8579

Phone: 530-752-0622

E-mail: jrpomeroy@ucdavis.edu

Website: http://ysp.ucdavis.edu

Program Type: Math, Sciences, Engineering, and Computer Science/Technology

Grade/Age Levels: Rising grades 11–12

Description: The UC Davis Young Scholars Program is a summer residential research program designed to expose 40 high-achieving high school sophomores and juniors to the world of original research in the natural sciences with emphases on the biological, environmental, and agricultural sciences. Participants in the UCD-YSP will work one-on-one with research faculty and research groups in state of the art laboratories for 6 weeks.

University of California–Irvine COSMOS

Contact: Mrs. Marjorie DeMartino, Director

Address: University of California-Irvine
Center for Educational Partnerships
420 Social Science Tower
Irvine, CA 92697-2505

Phone: 949-824-6806

Fax: 949-824-3048

E-mail: cosmos@uci.edu

Website: http://www.cosmos.uci.edu; http://www.ucop.edu/cosmos

Program Type: Math, Sciences, Engineering, and Computer Science/Technology

Grade/Age Levels: Grades 9–12

Description: The California State Summer School for Mathematics and Science (COSMOS) is a 4-week residential academic experience for top high school students in mathematics and science. Admission is by a competitive application process. The COSMOS courses address topics not traditionally taught in high schools: astronomy, genomics, robotics, tumor biology, and more. California residents may apply for need-based financial aid through the application process. COSMOS offers an exciting learning experience that features hands-on experimentation. It is an enrichment program; no credits given, neither are there exams or grades.

COSMOS is also offered at the following locations:

Description, Continued

- University of California, San Diego
  Jacobs School of Engineering
  9500 Gilman Dr., MC 0429
  La Jolla, CA 92093-0429
  858-822-4361
  858-822-3903 fax
  cosmos@ucsd.edu
  http://www.jacobsschool.ucsd.edu/cosmos

- University of California, Santa Cruz
  Attn: COSMOS
  Educational Partnership Center
  1156 High Street
  Santa Cruz, CA 95064
  831-459-1766
  831-459-3570 fax
  cosmos@ucsc.edu
  http://cosmos.ucsc.edu

- University of California, Davis
  COSMOS Program UC Davis
  1204 Mathematical Sciences Bldg.
  One Shields Ave.
  Davis, CA 95616
  530-754-7326
  530-754-7327 fax
  cosmos@ucdavis.edu
  http://cosmos.ucdavis.edu

University of Southern California Summer Programs

Contact: Sonny Hayes, Director

Address: University of Southern California
Summer Program Office
3601 Watt Way, GFS 304
Los Angeles, CA 90089-1695

Phone: 213-740-5679

Fax: 213-740-6417

E-mail: summer@usc.edu

Website: http://summer.usc.edu

Program Type: Academic Enrichment; Math, Sciences, Engineering, and Computer Science/ Technology; Fine, Performing, and Visual Arts

CALIFORNIA

Grade/Age Levels: Rising grades 10 and up

Description: USC Summer Programs offer high school students a preview of "freshman year" through 4- and 2-week summer courses. The 4-week courses offer three units of USC elective credit, and the 2-week, noncredit courses award students with a certificate of completion. Students may reside on campus for the full residential college experience, or local students may commute to campus daily. To be eligible, students must have completed at least the ninth grade by the start of the program and should be pursuing a rigorous high school curriculum. Graduating seniors are eligible to attend the summer before they begin college. The program is open to domestic and international students.

The Summer Programs academic schedule is intense and engaging; students take one course that meets Monday through Friday in a combination of lectures, discussions,

Description, Continued

hands-on workshops and labs, guest speakers and field trips to locations throughout Los Angeles. Supplementary workshops on the college application process and career planning allow students to take advantage of these expert resources available at USC. Evening and weekend recreational activities create a vibrant student community that completes the precollege experience.

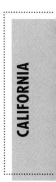

Center for Bright Kids Luminary Project

Contact: Dr. Amy Rushneck, Executive Director

Address: Center for Bright Kids
7705 Wadsworth Blvd, Unit F #300
Arvada, CO 80003

Phone: 303-428-2634

Fax: 303-428-2638

E-mail: cbk@centerforbrightkids.org

Website: https://www.centerforbrightkids.org

Program Type: Academic Enrichment

Grade/Age Levels: Rising grades 8–11

Description: The Luminary Project is a 3-week residential program held on the Colorado School of Mines campus for mature rising 8th–11th graders. Students focus on one intensive course of study for 6½ hours a day that is an equivalent to one full year of honors level high school content or one semester of college content. Many schools consider these courses for high school credit, although CBK cannot guarantee this transfer. As much as students think hard in the accelerated courses, they play hard in this deepened residential experience. Many students find that lifelong friends are made during this program, and full community weekend activities and trips are part of an energetic, structured residence life program.

Crow Canyon Archaeology Camps

Contact: Enrollment Manager

Address: Crow Canyon Archaeological Center
23390 Rd. K
Cortez, CO 81321-9908

Phone: 970-565-8975 ext. 146

E-mail: summercamp@crowcanyon.org

Website: http://www.crowcanyon.org/index.php/programs-for-teens

Program Type: Academic Enrichment

Grade/Age Levels: Grades 6–12

Description: Students work with Crow Canyon archaeologists while receiving an introduction to archaeology and Southwestern prehistory. Middle school students take a one-week session; high school students may take either the one-week excavation course or the 3-week field school.

Keystone Mountain Adventures

Contact: Lisa Thatcher, Camp and Community Programs Coordinator

Address: Keystone Science School
Keystone Mountain Adventures
1050 Soda Ridge Rd.
Keystone, CO 80435

Phone: 970-468-2098

E-mail: lthatcher@keystonescienceschool.org

Website: http://www.keystonescienceschool.org

Program Type: Leadership/Service/Volunteer; Math, Sciences, Engineering, and Computer Science/Technology

Grade/Age Levels: Ages 12–18

Description: The Keystone Mountain Adventures program uses hands-on experiential education and the exciting adventures of the Colorado wilderness to create an experience that any adventurous 12 to 18-year-old would enjoy. In sessions of 1–2 weeks, students will spend time camping in the Colorado Rocky Mountains, rafting in the famous Brown's canyon on the Arkansas River, and rock climbing. Students will enjoy scenic surroundings and educational lessons in forest ecology, aquatic ecology, and geology.

Keystone Science School also offers summer youth programs for all ages. Visit the website to request a brochure, or to register for a session. The program also offers the Counselor Assistant Program, designed for teens 12–17 years old who have an interest and a desire to develop their leadership skills. Experience the Rockies with future leaders and take home an adventure you will never forget!

Summer Science Program-Colorado

Contact: Mr. Richard Bowdon, Executive Director

Address: Summer Science Program
108 Whiteberry Dr.
Cary, NC 27519

Phone: 866-728-0999

Fax: 954-862-3051

E-mail: info@summerscience.org

Website: http://www.summerscience.org

Program Type: Math, Sciences, Engineering, and Computer Science/Technology

Grade/Age Levels: Rising grades 11–12

Description: One of the longest running and most successful precollege enrichment programs, SSP offers motivated students an exciting immersion into real-world, hands-on science. Working in teams of three, students perform an astronomical research project from start to finish: They determine the orbit of an asteroid from their own observations, measurements, and software. College-level lectures in astronomy, physics, calculus, and programming provide the practical and theoretical tools for each student to understand what he or she is doing and why. Although the pace is challenging, the emphasis is on cooperation, not competition. This 6-week residential program includes behind-the-scenes field trips to places like the Very Large Array. SSP takes place at two campuses: New Mexico Tech in Socorro, NM, and The University of Colorado in Boulder. The curriculum is identical at each.

Summer Study at Colorado State University

Address: Summer Study Programs
900 Walt Whitman Rd.
Melville, NY 11747

Phone: 631-424-1000

Fax: 631-424-0567

E-mail: info@summerstudy.com

Website: http://www.summerstudy.com/

Program Type: Academic Enrichment; Math, Sciences, Engineering, and Computer Science/Technology; Leadership/Service/Volunteer

Grade/Age Levels: Rising grades 9–11

Description: Summer Study at Colorado State University offers choices between 2-week, 3-week, and 4-week precollege programs that provide an exciting summer amidst the grandeur of the Rocky Mountains. Students completing 9th, 10th, or 11th grade are eligible for the unique opportunity to experience college life in a "nonpressured" atmosphere, where crucial life skills including time management, independence, and community-style living flourish. Students can take a variety of career exploration classes, community-service-based workshops, The Princeton Review SAT Prep with ACT Boost, and more.

University of Northern Colorado Summer Enrichment Program

Address: Summer Enrichment Program
University of Northern Colorado
Campus Box 141
Greeley, CO 80639

Phone: 970-351-2683

Fax: 970-351-1061

E-mail: sep@unco.edu

Website: http://www.unco.edu/sep

Program Type: Academic Enrichment

Grade/Age Levels: Rising grades 5–10

Description: The Summer Enrichment Program is a 2-week residential program for gifted, talented, creative, and high-ability learners entering 5th through 10th grades. Students will participate in stimulating academic experiences and fun social activities developed by gifted education specialists. Classes in this popular, affordable program are held on the UNC campus and trained counselors provide supervision during all nonclass time.

Yunasa West (Colorado)

Contact: Yunasa West Program Coordinator

Address: Institute for Educational Advancement–Yunasa
569 S. Marengo Ave.
Pasadena, CA 91101

Phone: 626-403-8900

Fax: 626-403-8905

E-mail: yunasa@educationaladvancement.org

Website: http://www.educationaladvancement.org

Program Type: Leadership/Service/Volunteer

Grade/Age Levels: Ages 10–14

Description: The Institute for Educational Advancement (IEA) is an independent, national nonprofit that matches gifted children with customized educational programs designed to serve their complex intellectual and personal needs. Located in Sedalia, CO, IEA's Yunasa West is a weeklong camp that unites highly able youngsters with experts in the social and emotional development of gifted children. In a nurturing setting, campers explore and grow the intellectual, spiritual, emotional, social, and physical aspects of their lives.

The camp offers guided imagery sessions, yoga, and traditional camp activities, as well as a wide variety of workshops focusing on topics such as teambuilding, leadership skills, and character building. The emphasis of all activities is on achieving balance, reminding campers that they are more than just intellect.

Every camper will learn techniques for integrating all aspects of their lives through small-group workshops led by Yunasa West's esteemed faculty. These experts have years of experience working with gifted youth and shaping gifted discourse in the U.S. through education, curriculum development, psychology practice, research, and writing.

Description, Continued

Yunasa West offers campers an opportunity to build community with like-minded peers, escape their busy everyday schedules, challenge themselves to develop into their personal best, gain self-acceptance, make lifelong friends, and have fun!

COLORADO

Academy Introduction Mission (AIM)

Address: United States Coast Guard Academy
Director of Admissions (AIM)
31 Mohegan Ave.
New London, CT 06320

Phone: 860-444-8503

Fax: 860-701-6700

E-mail: admissions@uscga.edu

Website: http://www.uscga.edu/AIM

Program Type: Math, Sciences, Engineering, and Computer Science/Technology

Grade/Age Levels: Rising grade 12

Description: AIM is a challenging summer program for students preparing to enter their senior year of high school who are interested in serving their country and exploring technical degree programs. For 6 action-packed days, students are immersed in Coast Guard tradition and Academy life in the classroom, in the engineering lab, on the playing fields, on the parade grounds, and on the water.

Center for Creative Youth at Wesleyan University

Contact: Lisa Foss, Program Coordinator

Address: Center for Creative Youth
at Wesleyan University
15 Vernon St.
Hartford, CT 06106

Phone: 860-757-6391 (Winter);
860-685-3307 (Summer)

E-mail: ccy@crec.org

Website: http://www.crec.org/ccy

Program Type: Fine, Performing, and Visual Arts;
Leadership/Service/Volunteer

Grade/Age Levels: Grades 10–12

Description: This 4-week residential program for pre-college students emphasizes the following creative areas: creative writing, dance, musical theater, filmmaking, music (vocal and instrumental), photography, theater, and visual arts.

National Computer Camps

Contact: Michael P. Zabinski, Ph.D., Executive Director

Address: National Computer Camps, Inc.
102 Shorefront
Milford, CT 06460

Phone: 203-710-5771

Fax: 203-254-4277

E-mail: info@nccamp.com

Website: http://www.nccamp.com

Program Type: Math, Sciences, Engineering, and Computer Science/Technology

Grade/Age Levels: Ages 7–18

Description: National Computer Camps (NCC) is America's original computer camp since 1977. The focus of NCC is Android App programming, 2D and 3D video game design, computer programming, digital video production, webpage design, 3D printing, A+ and Network+ certification, and software applications including networking, animation, Flash, and graphics. We offer all levels of programming in Basic, C++, Java, Assembler, HTML, XML, OpenGL, and JavaScript.

What distinguishes NCC from other camps is that NCC aims to teach youngsters ages 7–18 lifelong computer skills by providing a solid foundation in programming, focusing on languages, 2D and 3D game design, applications, and digital video editing. NCC is not a summer school, but rather a place where learning and fun are rolled into one and where the campers' self-esteem is of foremost importance. The camp is for youngsters of all levels of experience from beginner to advanced. In addition to computers, the campers enjoy an optional sports program. NCC has locations in Atlanta, GA; Fairfield, CT; Riverdale, NY; and Cleveland, OH.

Project Oceanology

Address: Project Oceanology
University of Connecticut
Avery Point Campus
1084 Shennecossett Rd.
Groton, CT 06340

Phone: 860-445-9007; 800-364-8472

Fax: 860-449-8008

E-mail: projecto@oceanology.org

Website: http://www.oceanology.org/kidsprogram.html

Program Type: Math, Sciences, Engineering, and Computer Science/Technology

Grade/Age Levels: Grades 4–12

Description: Project Oceanology camps include time aboard its Enviro-Lab research vessels and fleet of small boats, as well as exploration of near-shore habitats. Project Oceanology offers the following programs:

» *Ocean Camp*: Students, divided in groups for grades 5–12 and introduced to progressive learning levels at each grade, dive into a weeklong residential camp of hands-on, brains-on marine science. Students explore near-shore habitats of salt marshes, rocky intertidal zones and sandy beaches, and cruise the waters of Long Island Sound while conducting oceanographic research.

» *Ocean Explorer Academy*: Students in grades 4–6 roll up their sleeves, get their hands wet and have fun at a weeklong day camp. They discover the vital role habitats play in coastal ecosystems by using scientific instruments, such as trawl and plankton nets and water chemistry kits.

Description, Continued

- *Summer Marine Studies*: Students in grades 7–12 conduct scientific research and contribute to coastal fisheries' management plans at this 3-week day camp. As part of a research team supervised by marine scientists, students investigate marine life and present their findings.
- *Ocean Diversity Institute*: Students in grades 8–12 become part of a team conducting in-depth oceanographic research at this 3-week residential camp that explores the diversity of ecosystems, as well as that of camp participants. Students investigate marine life and present their findings.

Summer Institute for the Gifted (SIG)

CONNECTICUT

Address: Summer Institute for the Gifted
1 High Ridge Park
Stamford, CT 06905

Phone: 866-303-4744 ext. 5545

Fax: 203-399-5202

E-mail: sig.info@giftedstudy.com

Website: http://www.giftedstudy.com

Program Type: Academic Enrichment

Grade/Age Levels: Ages 5–17

Description: Summer Institute for the Gifted has three program types to choose from: residential, day, and commuter programs. The programs are designed for those students who are still open to the exploration of topics with which they may not be familiar. The formula is simple: take an amazing location, add a layer of strong academics in a risk-free forum, followed by a sprinkling of social opportunities and cultural awareness, and you end up with amazing SIGnificance! To qualify for admission, students must show eligibility as described on our website. A sampling of SIG's program locations is Princeton, Yale, University of Miami, and UC Berkeley. SIG is located on 9 college campuses and at 16 day locations. Programs are 3 weeks in duration and run at various times from June through August.

University of Delaware Edge Pre-College Experience

Contact: Kevin Liedel, Program Coordinator

Address: Edge
University of Deleware
186 S. College Ave.
Newark, DE 19716-7202

Phone: 302-831-6560

Fax: 302-831-4194

E-mail: edge@udel.edu

Website: http://www.udel.edu/edge

Program Type: Academic Enrichment

Grade/Age Levels: Rising grades 11–12

Description: This program offers a 5-week residential precollege experience for academically talented rising high school juniors and seniors. By emphasizing academic excellence, practical skill building, and student leadership, Edge offers young people the challenge, independence, and excitement of a living and learning experience that can only be found at a top national university. Students will live together in a residence hall; take two college-level courses for up to seven transferrable credits; participate in workshops to learn about university resources, writing and research techniques, and the college application process; complete a blog-based capstone project on service and leadership; and visit various cultural and historical locations in Delaware and the surrounding region.

The Catholic University of America Pre-College Programs

Address: CUA Summer
The Catholic University of America
330 Pangborn Hall
Washington, DC 20064

Phone: 202-319-5257

Fax: 202-319-6725

E-mail: cua-cuasummer@cua.edu

Website: http://summer.cua.edu/precollege

Program Type: Academic Enrichment; Fine, Performing, and Visual Arts; Math, Sciences, Engineering, and Computer Science/Technology

Grade/Age Levels: Grades 9–12

Description: The Catholic University of America's Summer Pre-College Programs allow students to become immersed in college life.

The Experiences in Architecture program is an intensive 3-week architecture workshop in which students tour design firms and construction sites and create models and drawings. Students are exposed to both the academic and the professional sides of the architecture arena as the city of Washington, DC, becomes their classroom.

Engineering New Frontiers is a weeklong residential camp for rising high school juniors and seniors. Students will work closely with CUA engineering faculty members to explore the wide variety of engineering opportunities in our society. Through classes, demonstrations, hands-on experiments, and field trips to various engineering local facilities, students will experience what college engineering majors and professional engineers do.

Description, Continued

The High School Summer Drama Institute is a 2-week residential drama program for rising juniors and seniors who wish to pursue a serious summer drama training experience. Students live on campus, attend daily classes, prepare monologues for auditions, attend theatre performances, and explore Washington, DC.

Discover the World of Communication

Contact: Sarah Menke-Fish, Assistant Professor and Director, Discover the World of Communication

Address: American University
School of Communication
4400 Massachusetts Ave. NW,
MGC 300
Washington, DC 20016

Phone: 205-885-2098

Fax: 202-885-2019

E-mail: audiscover@gmail.com

Website: http://www.american.edu/soc/discover

Program Type: Fine, Performing, and Visual Arts

Grade/Age Levels: Grades 9–12

Description: Build a digital portfolio, write a script, shoot and edit a film, write a news story like a pro, speak with confidence, persuade, inform, educate, and entertain. Choose from 35 professional, hands-on workshops that are open to students entering grades 9–12 and are taught by American University School of Communication faculty and communication professionals. Workshops include 16 mm film, 35 mm photography, Backpack Journalism, Social Media 101, Weather Broadcasting, Animation, Directing and Acting for the Camera, Special Effects, Video Game Design, Speaking for Impact, and many more. The length of the program is 2–4 weeks.

Science and Engineering Apprenticeship Program (SEAP)

Address: American Society for Engineering Education
Science and Engineering Apprenticeship Program
1818 N. St. NW, Ste. 600
Washington, DC 20036

Phone: 202-350-5765

E-mail: seap@asee.org

Website: http://seap.asee.org

Program Type: Internships/Paid Positions; Math, Sciences, Engineering, and Computer Science/Technology

Grade/Age Levels: Rising grades 10 and up

Description: This program offers various scientific, engineering, and math research studies at various locations. Students are encouraged to apply on site. The SEAP office places academically talented students in Department of Navy (DON) laboratories for 8 continuous weeks during the summer. These students, who usually possess a diverse background and have interest in sciences and mathematics, work closely with scientists and engineers who act as their mentors. The program offers students a unique and positive experience in their fields of interest, thus encouraging them to pursue careers in science and engineering.

Seacamp

Contact: Marketing Department

Address: Seacamp Association, Inc.
1300 Big Pine Ave.
Big Pine Key, FL 33043

Phone: 305-872-2331; 877-SEACAMP

Fax: 305-872-2555

E-mail: info@seacamp.org

Website: http://www.seacamp.org

Program Type: Math, Sciences, Engineering, and Computer Science/Technology

Grade/Age Levels: Ages 12–17

Description: Seacamp Association has operated since 1966, and is a nonprofit marine science education program located on Big Pine Key in the tropical Florida Keys and is accredited by the American Camp Association. The property is within the boundaries of the Florida Keys National Marine Sanctuary, the Coupon Bight Aquatic Preserve, the National Key Deer Refuge, and the Great White Heron National Wildlife Refuge.

During the summer, Seacamp offers two 18-day camp sessions and two 7-day camp sessions for teens 12–17. The program offers classes in marine science, as well as opportunities for SCUBA, windsurfing, sailing, kayaking, snorkeling, lifeguarding, and creative expressions, as well as other programs. Campers create their own daytime schedule and select from a wide range of marine science, SCUBA, aquatics, or creative expressions courses offered each session. Evening programs are a mix of activities for the whole camp, and may include campfires, dances, movies, science labs, and guest speakers. The two 7-day programs have program and SCUBA restrictions.

Description, Continued

As the only marine science summer camp with access to the Florida Keys National Marine Sanctuary, Seacamp is uniquely positioned to offer students amazing summer experiences through experiential education. Introductory classes provide an overview and a foundation for learning; intermediate classes provide coverage of more specific topics; Advanced classes offer opportunities for in-depth study and independent projects. Programs explore unique underwater environments, including spectacular coral reefs, sponge flats, seagrass meadows, tide pools, and shallow bays, all teeming with fascinating marine life.

A number of SCUBA classes are offered. Opportunities for the NAUI Diver Certification and the NAUI Master SCUBA Diver Certification provide a unique setting whereby teens can learn diving with other teens in a tropical environment. If campers are already certified, many courses are offered to continue their marine science education.

University of Miami Summer Scholars Program

Address: University of Miami
Summer Scholars Program
P.O. Box 248005
Coral Gables, FL 33124-1610

Phone: 305-284-5078

Website: http://www.miami.edu/ssp

E-mail: ssp@miami.edu

Program Type: Academic Enrichment

Grade/Age Levels: Grades 10–11

Description: The Summer Scholars Program is for current high school sophomores and juniors who have a minimum 3.0 grade point average and who are active in their communities, leaders in their schools, and examples of integrity. In this 3-week program, students earn college academic credit, interact with world-class professors, make lasting friendships, and grow as independent thinkers. Students choose an academic track based on their interest, take part in numerous hands-on activities, participate in educational field trips, and experience college life as a residential or commuter student.

Habitat for Humanity's Learn and Build Experience

Address: Habitat for Humanity International
121 Habitat St.
Americus, GA 31709-3498

Phone: 1-800-HABITAT ext. 2412

E-mail: youthprograms@habitat.org

Website: http://www.habitat.org/youthprograms

Program Type: Leadership/Service/Volunteer

Grade/Age Levels: Ages 16–18

Description: Habitat for Humanity's youth programs seek to engage young people in Habitat's mission to provide, safe, decent, and affordable shelter for some of the 1.6 billion people around the world who live in poverty housing. Learn and Build Experience trips, open to high school students, ages 16–18, provide hands-on education and community activities from raising the walls of a new house to cooking nightly dinners. Participants arrive individually to meet with 15 other students as strangers and leave with many friends, an appreciative partner family, and priceless memories. Visit the website to learn more about Learn and Build Experience trip locations and other Habitat for Humanity youth programs.

Savannah College of Art and Design (SCAD) Summer Seminars

Address: Summer Seminars
Savannah College of Art and Design
Admission Department
P.O. Box 2072
Savannah, GA 31402-2072

Phone: 800-869-7223

E-mail: atlantasss@scad.edu; savannahsss@scad.edu

Website: http://scad.edu/sss

Program Type: Fine, Performing, and Visual Arts

Grade/Age Levels: Rising grades 10–12

Description: SCAD Summer Seminars are residential or nonresidential summer workshops in Savannah and Atlanta designed for high school students who have completed their freshman, sophomore, or junior years. Topics include animation, digital photography, drawing, fashion, painting, and sequential art. Students can choose to live in a college residence hall, where they will receive meals on the college meal plan.

Spelman College Summer Programs

Address: Summer Programs
Spelman College
350 Spelman Lane SW, Box 849
Atlanta, GA 30314-4399

Phone: 404-270-5184

Website: http://www.spelman.edu/academics/summer-programs

Program Type: Math, Sciences, Engineering, and Computer Science/Technology; Academic Enrichment

Grade/Age Levels: Grades 10–12

Description: The College Prep Institute (CPI) is a 2-week residential college preparatory program for female high school students who are college-bound rising sophomores and juniors. CPI features hands-on seminars, college preparation workshops, online sessions, and lessons with homework and test preparation.

The Early College Program (ECP) is a residential program for female high school students who are college-bound rising juniors, rising seniors, or graduating seniors. ECP is an intense academic program that offers college credit courses in English or biology for current high school juniors and seniors. A noncredit STEM module is another option, which is also open to high school sophomores and features interactive lectures, quantitative research analysis, group projects, report writing, and field trips.

Hawaii Preparatory Academy Summer Session

Contact: Shirley Ann Fukumoto, Assistant Headmaster and Summer Session Principal

Address: Hawaii Preparatory Academy
Summer Session
65-1692 Kohala Mountain Road
Kamuela, HI 96743-8476

Phone: 808-881-4088

Fax: 808-881-4045

E-mail: summer@hpa.edu

Website: http://www.hpa.edu/summer

Program Type: Academic Enrichment

Grade/Age Levels: Grades 6–12

Description: Summer at Hawaii Preparatory Academy (HPA) on the island of Hawaii offers students a unique 4-week boarding experience structured for academic enrichment and designed to make the most of the summer and take advantage of the wondrous island—home to 80% of the world's ecosystems.

Summer Session students select three 2-hour classes and participate in an after-school sport from 3:30 p.m. to 5 p.m. Many offerings focus on sustainable living integrated into language arts, math, science, visual arts, and Hawaiian culture classes. Students in grades 9–12 may select one of two credit courses in marine science or environmental stewardship.

Summer at HPA offers new and prospective HPA students an excellent introduction to the school's program and instructors. Many students return every summer to take advantage of the outstanding program and staff and to meet students from around the world.

Junior Engineering, Math and Science (JEMS) Summer Workshop

Address: University of Idaho
College of Engineering
875 Perimeter Drive MS 1011
Moscow, ID 83844-1011

Phone: 208-885-6470

E-mail: deanengr@uidaho.edu

Website: http://www.uidaho.edu/jems

Program Type: Math, Sciences, Engineering, and Computer Science/Technology

Grade/Age Levels: Rising grade 12

Description: The University of Idaho College of Engineering sponsors the annual Idaho Junior Engineering, Mathematics, and Science (JEMS) Summer Workshop for students who have completed their junior year of high school. The focus of the workshop is to expose students to engineering problems within technical and social contexts, and to encourage them to enroll in college. Students will participate in lab exercises, field trips, computer exercises, and recreational activities. At the end of the workshop, participants will have a better grasp of basic engineering principles, a sharper focus on what to do in their college career, and a real connection with new friends.

Aerospace Institute Summer Camp

Contact: Ms. Diane Jeffers

Address: Aerospace Institute Summer Camp
University of Illinois at Urbana-Champaign
308 Talbot Laboratory
104 S. Wright St.
Urbana, IL 61801-2935

Phone: 217-244-8048

E-mail: dejeffer@illinois.edu

Website: http://isgc.aerospace.illinois.edu/iai

Program Type: Math, Sciences, Engineering, and Computer Science/Technology

Grade/Age Levels: Rising grades 9–12

Description: This one-week program for high school students offers classroom and hands-on experience in the areas of propulsion systems, theory of flight, aerodynamics, principles of aircraft, and spacecraft design. See website for additional programs.

CAA High School Field School

Contact:	Director of Education, Center for American Archeology
Address:	Center for American Archeology (CAA) P.O. Box 366 Kampsville, IL 62053
Phone:	618-653-4316
Fax:	618-653-4232
E-mail:	caa@caa-archeology.org
Website:	http://www.caa-archeology.org
Program Type:	Academic Enrichment
Grade/Age Levels:	Ages 13–17
Description:	In this youth field school, students learn the basics of archaeological field excavation, conduct lab work, and explore ancient technologies and skills. Real archaeology—really fun! Additional programs are listed on CAA website.

The Center for Gifted at National-Louis University Summer Programs

Contact:	Ms. Joan Smutny, Director
Address:	The Center for Gifted at National-Louis University Box 364 Wilmette, IL 60091
Phone:	847-901-0173
Fax:	847-901-0179
E-mail:	info@centerforgifted.org
Website:	http://www.centerforgifted.org
Program Type:	Academic Enrichment
Grade/Age Levels:	Grades K–10
Description:	The Center for Gifted at National-Louis University offers many opportunities for gifted children to explore diverse subjects in a challenging, creative environment, free from pressures of tests and grades, where each child's unique talents and gifts are sensitively nurtured. Creativity and critical thinking are inherent in all classes and activities and compromise the framework for teaching. Courses are available for children in kindergarten through grade 10 at many Chicago area locations and at two National-Louis University campuses.

Center for Talent Development (CTD) Summer Program

Address: Summer Program
Center for Talent Development
Northwestern University
617 Dartmouth Pl.
Evanston, IL 60208

Phone: 847-491-3782, ext. 2

Fax: 847-467-0880

E-mail: summer@ctd.northwestern.edu

Website: http://www.ctd.northwestern.edu/summer

Program Type: Academic Enrichment; Math, Sciences, Engineering, and Computer Science/Technology; Foreign Language

Grade/Age Levels: Grades 4–12

Description: Do you want to complete AP Calculus in just 3 weeks? Are you eager to combine rigorous and engaging academic work with community service and hands-on field experiences designed to help young people develop the knowledge, experience, and leadership skills they need to make a positive impact on society?

Students completing grades 4–12 may sign up for 1–3-week sessions during which they can take one course. More than 100 enrichment, honors, and Advanced Placement courses are included.

Students grades 4 and above may reside on Northwestern University's Evanston campus. Classes are held daily from 8:30 a.m. to 2:45 p.m. Weekends are spent exploring Chicago's cultural offerings. Civic Leadership Institute participants live in Chicago.

Exploring Your Options and Discover Engineering

Address: Worldwide Youth in Science and Engineering
206 Engineering Hall
1308 W. Green St.
Urbana, IL 61801

Phone: 217-244-3517

E-mail: wyse@illinois.edu

Website: https://wyse.engineering.illinois.edu

Program Type: Math, Sciences, Engineering, and Computer Science/Technology

Grade/Age Levels: Rising grades 10–12

Description: Exploring Your Options (EYO) is a one-week residential camp that provides students who are interested in math and science a chance to visit and participate in hands-on activities in each of the departments in the College of Engineering. Two sessions are offered and the camps are limited to 40 students each. Exploring Your Options is for students who will be in the 11th or 12th grade in the fall of the current calendar year.

Discover Engineering is a one-week residential camp for rising sophomores who are interested in math and science. Students will work on several projects that will incorporate different aspects of engineering. The camp is limited to 30 students. Discover Engineering is for students who will be in the 10th grade in the fall of the current calendar year.

Girls' Adventures in Math, Engineering, and Science (GAMES) Camp

Contact: Ms. Angela Wolters

Address: GAMES Summer Camp
Women in Engineering Program
University of Illinois at Urbana-Champaign
210A Engineering Hall, MC-272
1308 W. Green St.
Urbana, IL 61801

Phone: 217-244-3517

Fax: 217-244-4974

E-mail: engr-games@illinois.edu

Website: https://publish.illinois.edu/womeninengineering/camps/g-a-m-e-s-camp

Program Type: Math, Sciences, Engineering, and Computer Science/Technology

Grade/Age Levels: Rising grades 9–12

Description: GAMES is an annual summer camp designed to give academically talented high school-aged girls an opportunity to explore exciting engineering and scientific fields through demonstrations, classroom presentations, hands-on activities, and contacts with women in these technical fields. We currently offer eight different engineering tracks open to different grade levels: aerospace (9th–12th), bioengineering (9th–11th), chemical engineering (9th–12th), computer science (9th–12th), environmental engineering and sustainability (10th–12th), mechanical engineering (9th–12th), Girls Learning Electrical Engineering (GLEE; 10th–12th), and Girls Learning about Materials (GLAM; 10th–12th). The eight tracks are split up into one-week camps throughout the months of June and July.

Summer@IMSA

Address: Illinois Mathematics and Science Academy
1500 Sullivan Rd.
Aurora, IL 60506-1067

Phone: 630-907-5950

Fax: 630-907-5945

E-mail: summerprograms@imsa.edu

Website: https://www.imsa.edu/extensionprograms/summer_at_imsa

Program Type: Math, Sciences, Engineering, and Computer Science/Technology

Grade/Age Levels: Grades 3–10

Description: Science, technology, engineering, and mathematics (STEM) take center stage in Summer@IMSA programs. STEM topics are often integrated using real-world contexts, such as energy production or biotechnology. Programs are designed to foster an intellectually challenging and fun environment. Student learning activities focus on discovery, exploration, and problem-solving skills. Each program lasts approximately one week. Day programs include snack, lunch, T-shirt, and supplies. Residential camps include accommodations, meals, T-shirt, and supplies. Visit the website for an updated listing of programs.

National Student Leadership Conference (NSLC)

Contact: Mr. Rick Duffy, Executive Director

Address: National Student Leadership Conference
Office of Admissions
320 Ohio St., Ste. 4W
Chicago, IL 60654

Phone: 312-322-9999; 800-994-6752

Fax: 312-765-0081

E-mail: info@nslcleaders.org

Website: http://www.nslcleaders.org

Program Type: Academic Enrichment

Grade/Age Levels: Grades 9–12

Description: The National Student Leadership Conference offers high-achieving high school students the opportunity to explore a future career hands-on while developing essential leadership skills, experiencing life on a college campus, and interacting with a diverse group of students from across the U.S. and around the world.

During college-level lectures and interactive career simulations, students will gain insight into one of the following fields: medicine, engineering, law, business, biotechnology, forensic science, government and politics, international diplomacy, intelligence and national security, theater, sports management, culinary arts, or journalism and media arts.

Programs are held on college campuses around the U.S., including American University, Georgia Tech, Fordham University, Harvard Medical School, Northwestern University, the University of California, Berkeley, the University of Washington, and Yale University.

School of the Art Institute of Chicago Early College Program Summer Institute

Address: The School of the Art Institute of Chicago
36 S. Wabash Ave.
Chicago, IL 60603

Phone: 312-629-6170

Fax: 312-629-6171

E-mail: ecp@saic.edu

Website: http://www.saic.edu/ecp

Program Type: Fine, Performing, and Visual Arts

Grade/Age Levels: Grades 10–12

Description: The School of the Art Institute of Chicago offers intensive 2- and 4-week courses for high school students at least 15 years of age who have completed their sophomore, junior, or senior year. Housing, merit scholarships, and financial aid are available. Areas of study include animation, architecture, art and technology studies, drawing, exhibition and curatorial studies, fashion, film, video, graphic design, painting, photography, sculpture, writing, and more.

University of Chicago Summer Session

Address: The University of Chicago
The Graham School of Continuing Liberal and Professional Studies
1427 E. 60th St.
Chicago, IL 60637

Phone: 773-834-3792

E-mail: summerhs@uchicago.edu

Website: http://summer.uchicago.edu

Program Type: Math, Sciences, Engineering, and Computer Science/Technology; Fine, Performing, and Visual Arts; Gap Year/Study Abroad/International Travel; Foreign Language

Grade/Age Levels: Grades 9–12

Description: The University of Chicago offers the following summer programs:

» *Intensive Subject Courses*: In these 3-week courses, students are able to join experts in various fields to have an experiential learning opportunity.

» *Research in the Biological Sciences*: Experience "life at the bench" and learn cutting-edge molecular, cellular, and microbiological research techniques.

» *Stones and Bones*: Join the Field Museum of Natural History's Lance Grande on an expedition digging for fossils.

» *Rocky Mountain Ecology*: A unique field experience in Wyoming, focusing on the relationships in the UNESCO World Heritage Site of the Greater Yellowstone Ecosystem.

Description, Continued

- *Summer Quarter for High School Students*: Take intensive language study or other courses from the regular college curriculum, and study alongside undergraduates from the University of Chicago and elsewhere.
- *Traveling Academy*: Travel to Greece to study the role of drama and performance in ancient Greek culture.

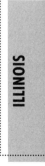

Ball State University College of Architecture and Planning's DesignWorks Summer Academy

Contact: Ms. Melanie Smith

Address: Ball State University
College of Architecture and Planning
Attn: DesignWorks Summer Academy
Muncie, IN 47306

Phone: 765-285-5862

E-mail: msmith@bsu.edu

Website: http://cms.bsu.edu/academics/collegesanddepartments/cap/summer-academy/admissions

Program Type: Fine, Performing, and Visual Arts

Grade/Age Levels: Grades 10–12

Description: Each spring, the College of Architecture and Planning invites outstanding high school juniors and seniors to apply for admission to the DesignWorks Summer Studio. This workshop is an intensive immersion into the realm of environmental design and problem solving. CAP faculty members bring this program to the participants via a series of exercises that increasingly challenge the young mind and its understanding of the built environment. The exercises are designed to encourage exploration and growth of creativity and uniqueness found in each individual personality.

Ball State University Summer Journalism Workshops

Contact: Mr. Brian Hayes

Address: Ball State University
Department of Journalism Secondary Education Services
2000 W. University Ave.
Muncie, IN 47306

Phone: 765-285-8900

Fax: 765-285-7997

E-mail: bsuworkshops@bsu.edu

Website: http://www.bsujournalismworkshops.com

Program Type: Fine, Performing, and Visual Arts

Grade/Age Levels: Grades 8–12

Description: Nearly 400 high school journalists and media publication advisers come to campus each July for Ball State's annual summer journalism workshops. The Department of Journalism's Secondary Education Services office, which also runs Junior High Journalism Day each fall and High School Journalism Day each spring, plans the summer events. The week-long summer workshops allow students to study specific areas of journalism with award-winning journalists and publication advisers. The workshop offers a wide array of courses in newspaper, yearbook, magazine, broadcast, online, social, and emerging media platforms.

Gifted Education Resource Institute (GERI) at Purdue University

Contact: Dr. Marcia Gentry, Director, GERI

Address: 100 N. University St.
Beering Hall, Room 5178
West Lafayette, IN 47907-1446

Phone: 765-494-7243

Fax: 765-496-2706

E-mail: geri@purdue.edu

Website: http://geri.education.purdue.edu

Program Type: Academic Enrichment; Math, Sciences, Engineering, and Computer Science/Technology; Fine, Performing, and Visual Arts

Grade/Age Levels: Grades 5–12

Description: Since 1977, GERI Summer Residential Camps have offered gifted, creative, and talented students challenging and enjoyable academic experiences combined with a wide variety of cultural, athletic, and recreational options. Each July, Summer Residential students (grades 5–12) stay in air-conditioned residence halls, engage in challenging courses taught by outstanding educators, and enjoy a wide variety of social and recreational activities planned by their camp counselors. Comet students (grades 5 and 6) enroll for 1–2 weeks; whereas Star (grades 7 and 8) and Pulsar (grades 9–12) students enroll for 2–4 weeks. Students explore their areas of interests in a college atmosphere where they study topics typically not offered in school, and they have access to all of the resources of Purdue University, a leading Big 10 research university.

Introduction to Engineering

Contact: Ramzi Bualuan, IEP Director

Address: Introduction to Engineering
University of Notre Dame
384 Fitzpatrick Hall of Engineering
Notre Dame, IN 46556

Phone: 574-631-6092

Fax: 574-631-9260

E-mail: iep@nd.edu

Website: http://iep.nd.edu

Program Type: Math, Sciences, Engineering, and Computer Science/Technology

Grade/Age Levels: Rising grade 12

Description: Introduction to Engineering is a 2-week summer program for high school students. Students are given a taste of college life while discovering career opportunities in engineering and receiving an overview of the elements of engineering design and computer programming. Cost includes regular field trips, incidentals, meal plans, and housing.

Operation Catapult

Contact: Ms. Lisa Norton, Dean of Admissions

Address: Operation Catapult
Rose-Hulman Institute of Technology
5500 Wabash Ave.
Terre Haute, IN 47803

Phone: 800-248-7448

Fax: 812-877-8941

E-mail: lisa.norton@rose-hulman.edu

Website: http://www.rose-hulman.edu/catapult

Program Type: Math, Sciences, Engineering, and Computer Science/Technology

Grade/Age Levels: Grade 11 only

Description: This 3-week residential camp allows students to work on an engineering or science-related project with experienced faculty and current students. While living on campus with an extensive social program, students will have a once-in-a-lifetime experience at Operation Catapult.

OPTIONS

Contact: Tina Newman, Coordinator, Summer OPTIONS Programs

Address: University of Evansville
College of Engineering and Computer Science
1800 Lincoln Ave.
Evansville, IN 47722

Phone: 812-488-2570

E-mail: vh12@evansville.edu

Website: http://www.evansville.edu/options

Program Type: Math, Sciences, Engineering, and Computer Science/Technology; Gap Year/Study Abroad/International Travel

Grade/Age Levels: Grades 9–11; Grades 6–8

Description: OPTIONS for High School Girls is an all-inclusive residential camp for high-school-aged girls who have passed geometry and will be in grades 10–12 in the fall or the equivalent homeschooled level. Students take challenging courses with university professors and job shadow professional female engineers and computer scientists as part of this program.

OPTIONS for Middle School Girls is a day program in which students experience confidence-building and team-building activities. STEM-based classes are taught by current engineering and computer science students, who also serve as counselors. Professional women in these fields also teach classes.

Iowa State University Office of Precollegiate Programs for Talented and Gifted (OPPTAG)

IOWA

Address: Iowa State University
357 Carver Hall
Ames, IA 50011-2060

Phone: 515-294-1772

E-mail: opptag@iastate.edu

Website: http://www.opptag.iastate.edu

Program Type: Academic Enrichment

Grade/Age Levels: Grades 3–12

Description: Iowa State University's OPPTAG offers academic enrichment through Explorations and Adventures. During these programs students explore, observe, discover, question, scrutinize, evaluate, and ponder fascinating subjects such as art, astronomy, chemistry, computer science, history, literature, engineering, and psychology, along with other gifted students from Iowa, the V.S., and even across the globe. The program is for students interested in accelerated, fast-paced academic courses.

Explorations (for students entering grades 9–11) will appeal to you if you are intrigued by discovering new and exciting areas of study not traditionally taught in the high school curriculum. Each one-week voyage will offer you an enriched learning experience, introduce you to cutting-edge concepts within a topic area, be student focused, and immerse you in activities and laboratories designed to stimulate your thinking skills and encourage you to continue your personal adventure in learning. Explorations

Description, Continued

is a residential community of gifted students learning and connecting outside of the classroom, as well. Evening activities include everything from swimming and painting, to trivia, design contests, and more!

Adventures will give younger students (entering grades 3–6, 7–8) the opportunity to explore the worlds of science, ancient civilizations, math, art, literature, reading, and engineering led by qualified faculty. Adventures is full of hands-on lessons, exiting discoveries, and a lot of FUN!

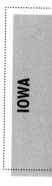

Secondary Student Training Program (SSTP)

Contact:	Dr. Lori Ihrig or Ms. Jan Warren
Address:	Belin-Blank Center 600 Blank Honors Center University of Iowa Iowa City, IA 52242
Phone:	319-335-6148 or 800-336-6463
Fax:	319-335-5151
E-mail:	lori-ihrig@uiowa.edu; janwarren@uiowa.edu
Website:	http://sstpuiowa.wordpress.com
Program Type:	Academic Enrichment; Math, Sciences, Engineering, and Computer Science/ Technology
Grade/Age Levels:	Rising grades 11–12
Description:	Students may apply for the Secondary Student Training Program (SSTP), a 6-week residential summer research program at the University of Iowa. Students will conduct research in university laboratories under the guidance of a faculty mentor. Additionally, students will take an evening class and attend a weekly seminar series. Students will also produce a research abstract and academic poster. Through SSTP, students earn 3 semester hours of university credit.

Exploring Science Technology & Engineering (EXCITE!)

Contact: Ms. Sara Heiman, Program Coordinator

Address: Exploring Science Technology & Engineering
Kansas State University
125 Seaton Hall
Manhattan, KS 66506

Phone: 785-532-6088

Fax: 785-532-2627

E-mail: kawse@ksu.edu

Website: http://www.k-state.edu/excite

Program Type: Math, Sciences, Engineering, and Computer Science/Technology

Grade/Age Levels: Grades 9–12

Description: EXCITE! is designed to foster girls' continuing interest in STEM. EXCITE offers programs throughout the academic year to let students visit K-State's campus in Manhattan, KS, and meet undergraduate students and faculty in STEM disciplines. In the summer, students participate in a 3-day workshop and learn about the latest research through hands-on activities presented by undergraduate and graduate students and faculty.

The Center for Gifted Studies Summer Programs

Contact:	Julia Roberts, Director
Address:	The Center for Gifted Studies Western Kentucky University 1906 College Heights Blvd #71031 Bowling Green, KY 42101-1031
Phone:	270-745-6323
Fax:	270-745-6279
E-mail:	gifted@wku.edu
Website:	http://www.wku.edu/gifted
Program Type:	Academic Enrichment
Grade/Age Levels:	Rising grades 7–9
Description:	The Summer Camp for Academically Talented Middle School Students (SCATS) provides an opportunity for students entering grades 7–9 to spend 2 weeks participating in myriad cultural, educational, and recreational activities. Students select four classes from dozens of choices. Students may be nonresidential or residential; residential campers live in an air-conditioned residence hall. Counselors supervise evening and weekend activities. The Summer Program for Verbally and Mathematically Precocious Youth (VAMPY) is a 3-week program for students in grades 7–10. Content areas include astronomy, chemistry, genetics, humanities, mathematics, Nazi Germany and the Holocaust, and writing among others.

ADVANCE Program for Young Scholars

Contact: Ms. Harriette Palmer, Assistant Director

Address: ADVANCE Program
NSU Box 5671
Natchitoches, LA 71497

Phone: 318-357-4500

Fax: 318-357-4547

E-mail: palmerh@nsula.edu

Website: http://advance.nsula.edu

Program Type: Academic Enrichment

Grade/Age Levels: Rising grades 8–12

Description: The ADVANCE Program for Young Scholars at the Northwestern State University of Louisiana is a summer residential program that offers intensive, fast-paced courses in the humanities, mathematics, natural sciences, and computer science. Students selected to participate in ADVANCE enroll in one course during the 3-week term. By working with carefully selected instructors and teaching assistants, each student is given the opportunity to attain maximum academic growth. Classes are generally limited to 15 students. The residential life portion is an equally important aspect of the program and a wide array of extracurricular activities are offered each evening to encourage relaxation and socialization. ADVANCE is an affiliate program of the Duke University Talent Identification Program (TIP).

Camp Encore/Coda

Contact: Ms. Jamie Saltman, Owner and Director

Address: Camp Encore/Coda
32 Grassmere Rd.
Brookline, MA 02467

Phone: 617-325-1541

Fax: 617-325-7278

E-mail: jamie@encore-coda.com

Website: http://www.encore-coda.com

Program Type: Fine, Performing, and Visual Arts

Grade/Age Levels: Rising grade 9 and up

Description: This summer camp is held in Sweden, ME, each year and offers private musical training and ensemble training in everything from chamber music, to rock bands. High schoolers may be counselors in training and may also attend the traditional program or the conservatory program for more intensive musical experience. The camp also includes traditional activities like arts and crafts, sports, canoeing, swimming, and field trips.

Summer Address:
50 Encore/Coda Lane
Sweden, ME 04040
Phone: 207-647-3947
Fax: 207-647-3259

The Jackson Laboratory Summer Student Program

Contact: Michael McKernan, Summer Program Director

Address: Education Office
The Jackson Laboratory
610 Main St.
Bar Harbor, ME 04609

Phone: 207-288-6000

Fax: 207-288-6150

E-mail: summerstudents@jax.org

Website: http://education.jax.org/summerstudent/index.html

Program Type: Internships/Paid Positions; Math, Sciences, Engineering, and Computer Science/Technology

Grade/Age Levels: Grades 11–12

Description: An internationally recognized center for mammalian genetic research, The Jackson Laboratory is an independent nonprofit institution. Here, outstanding students conduct interdisciplinary biomedical research as apprentices in the laboratories of staff scientists. This program emphasizes methods of discovery and communication of new knowledge. Students also learn techniques, fundamentals, and ethics of biology, because these are essential in research. At the time of participation in the program, a high school student must have completed grade 11 or 12 and be at least 16 years old. Participants must be U.S. citizens or permanent residents. Students receive room and board and a stipend.

University of Maine Summer Youth Music

Contact: Christopher G. White, Director

Address: University of Maine Summer Youth Music
University of Maine
School of Performing Arts
5788 Class of 1944 Hall
Orono, ME 04469-5788

Phone: 207-581-4703

Fax: 207-581-4701

E-mail: music@maine.edu

Website: http://umaine.edu/spa/msym

Program Type: Fine, Performing, and Visual Arts

Grade/Age Levels: Rising Grades 6–12

Description: The University of Maine Summer Youth Music program offers two levels of study: Junior Camp and Senior Camp. Junior Camp is for students entering grades 6–8. Each junior camper will participate in symphonic band, concert band, chorus, or strings ensemble. Additional ensembles will include jazz bands and musical theatre. Campers may also participate in chamber ensembles, music classes, master classes, and piano and guitar instruction.

Senior Camp is for students entering grades 9–12. Each senior camper will participate in symphonic band, concert band, or chorus. Additional ensembles will include jazz bands, combos, and musical theatre. Senior campers may also participate in jazz improvisation, small ensembles, chamber groups, music classes, master classes, and piano and guitar instruction. A recreational activity is planned for midweek of camp, as well as other organized events, including concerts by faculty and students.

Young Artist Workshops

Address: Young Artist Workshops
P.O. Box 200
70 Camden St.
Rockport, ME 04856

Phone: 207-236-8581

E-mail: info@mainemedia.edu

Website: http://www.mainemedia.edu/workshops/young-artists

Program Type: Fine, Performing, and Visual Arts

Grade/Age Levels: Ages 14–17

Description: Each summer, a select group of high school students have the opportunity to spend one or 2 weeks studying and working in their chosen field of investigation: filmmaking, photography, multimedia, or design. The campus experience allows these high school students the opportunity to work alongside professionals, see their work, and listen to the world's most honored artists speak about their work and process.

Young artists' workshops in photography, filmmaking, animation, and more are available to high school students throughout the summer. Visit the website for a full listing of workshops and dates, or to download a course catalog.

Center for Talented Youth (CTY) Summer Programs

Contact: Dr. Elaine Hansen, Executive Director

Address: Johns Hopkins University
Center for Talented Youth
McAuley Hall
5801 Smith Ave., Ste 400
Baltimore, MD 21209

Phone: 410-735-6277

Fax: 866-345-3731

E-mail: ctyinfo@jhu.edu

Website: http://cty.jhu.edu/summer

Program Type: Academic Enrichment

Grade/Age Levels: Grades 2–12

Description: CTY summer program courses span a range of liberal arts disciplines, including language, history, writing, and the arts, as well as mathematics and science. All courses are challenging and are taught well above grade level. They cover a great deal of material and place emphasis on active learning and putting knowledge to use in independent and creative ways. Rather than assign grades, our instructors write detailed evaluations describing each student's progress and achievements in the course and outlining areas for further growth.

Exploring Engineering at the University of Maryland (E2@UMD) Program

Contact: Ms. Bria Barry, Assistant Director, Women in Engineering Program

Address: Exploring Engineering at the University of Maryland Program
University of Maryland
1131 Glenn L. Martin Hall
College Park, MD 20742

Phone: 301-405-3283

Fax: 301-314-9867

E-mail: bmcelroy@umd.edu

Website: http://www.wie.umd.edu/k12/e2atumd

Program Type: Math, Sciences, Engineering, and Computer Science/Technology

Grade/Age Levels: Rising grades 11–12

Description: Exploring Engineering at the University of Maryland (E2@UMD) is a one-week summer program for high school women (rising juniors or seniors) who are considering engineering as a possible major and career. You will live on campus for one week and explore the world of engineering through fun hands-on activities, laboratory experiments, informative workshops, team challenges, and seminars with professional engineers.

Maryland Institute College of Art Summer Pre-College

Address: Pre-College Program
Maryland Institute College of Art
1300 Mount Royal Ave.
Baltimore, MD 21217

Phone: 410-225-2219

Fax: 410-225-2229

E-mail: precollege@mica.edu

Website: http://www.mica.edu/precollege

Program Type: Fine, Performing, and Visual Arts

Grade/Age Levels: Rising grades 11–12

Description: This residential program offers the opportunity to earn three college credits, enhance your portfolio, and receive in-depth studio instruction, while experiencing college-level art study. Students receive workshop instruction in new media and art skills and complete an art history seminar. Limited financial assistance is available.

MICA's home base of Baltimore is at the heart of the New York–Washington, D.C. art corridor. Saturday trips during the residency program will let you explore nationally and internationally recognized art museums.

Stepping Stones to Your Future

Contact: Stepping Stones Camp Coordinator

Address: Stepping Stones to Your Future
University of Maryland
1131 Glenn L. Martin Hall
College Park, MD 20742

Phone: 301-405-0315

Fax: 301-314-9867

E-mail: Visit camp website

Website: http://wie.umd.edu/k12/sstyf

Program Type: Math, Sciences, Engineering, and Computer Science/Technology

Grade/Age Levels: Rising grades 7–8

Description: Stepping Stones to Your Future is an annual summer engineering camp for rising seventh and eighth graders, offered by the University of Maryland, College Park. This one-week commuter camp is an excellent opportunity for young men and women who are interested in science and engineering to work with current University of Maryland students on a variety of fun and hands-on engineering activities.

Summer Institute in Science, Technology, Engineering, and Research (SISTER)

Contact: Sarah Brown or Marian Carson

Address: Summer Institute in Science, Technology, Engineering, and Research
NASA/Goddard Space Flight Center
Education Office
Code 120
Greenbelt, MD 20771

Phone: 301-286-7262

E-mail: GSFC-SISTER@mail.nasa.gov

Website: http://education.gsfc.nasa.gov/sister#

Program Type: Math, Sciences, Engineering, and Computer Science/Technology

Grade/Age Levels: Rising grades 7–8

Description: SISTER, the Summer Institute in Science, Technology, Engineering, and Research at NASA Goddard Space Flight Center, is designed to increase awareness of and provide an opportunity for female middle school students to be exposed to and explore nontraditional career fields with GSFC women engineers, mathematicians, scientists, technicians, and researchers. The objectives of the program include introducing young women to a technical working environment; acquainting students with GSFC missions; providing an awareness of educational programs and internships available during high school, undergraduate, and graduate study; and providing observations and experiences with real hands-on projects researched and developed by women at GSFC. The program takes place for one week each year during the summer.

University of Maryland Jump Start Program

Contact: Dr. Kaci Thompson, Director

Address: Jump Start Program
1313 Symons Hall
College of Computer, Mathematical, and Natural Sciences
University of Maryland
College Park, MD 20742

Phone: 301-405-3353

E-mail: HHMI@umd.edu

Website: http://hhmi.umd.edu/outreach/jumpstart

Program Type: Math, Sciences, Engineering, and Computer Science/Technology

Grade/Age Levels: Grades 11–12

Description: This weeklong science immersion program allows commuter students to learn about the research process while working in the university's biology laboratories. Past programs have focused on forensic science, biomedical science, biotechnology, and animal physiology and behavior. Applications must be postmarked by March 15.

3D Game Design at Brandeis University

Contact: Joshua Mocle

Address: 3D Game Design
Brandeis University
415 South St.
MS 065
Waltham, MA 02454

Phone: 781-736-8416

Fax: 815-301-2874

E-mail: highschool@brandeis.edu

Website: http://www.brandeis.edu/highschool/3dgame

Program Type: Academic Enrichment; Math, Sciences, Engineering, and Computer Science/Technology

Grade/Age Levels: Rising grades 9–12

Description: As a participant in Brandeis's 3D Game Design, you will learn how to create your own 3D world using the Blender Game Design Platform. The program will give you the tools to design a variety of games including racing, questing, multiplayer competition and cooperation games, and games straight from your imagination. See your visions come alive in vivid, interactive 3D!

Along with building games, participants will explore the history of gaming and enjoy field trips around Greater Boston. Participants will live in Brandeis University dorms and build a community passionate about the world of 3D games. The program concludes with a 3D Game Design Festival where you will present your games to invited guests.

3D Game Design is one of several programs where passionate, motivated high school students immerse themselves in hands-on learning experiences while getting a taste of life on the Brandeis campus.

Adventures in Veterinary Medicine (AVM)

Address: Tufts University Cummings School of Veterinary Medicine
200 Westboro Rd.
North Grafton, MA 01536

Phone: 508-839-7962

Fax: 508-839-7952

E-mail: AVM@tufts.edu

Website: http://www.tufts.edu/vet/avm

Program Type: Academic Enrichment

Grade/Age Levels: Grades 9–12

Description: The Adventures in Veterinary Medicine High School Program is an engaging and fun way for high school students to spend 2 weeks learning more about the veterinary profession. This is your opportunity to dig into veterinary medicine through an exciting and intensive program where you'll be surrounded by others who share your passion for animals, health, and science. You will:

- » Explore specialty fields and important topics in veterinary medicine through informative lectures by Tufts faculty, staff, and vet students.
- » See what it's really like to be a vet as you shadow fourth-year veterinary students in the Foster Hospital for Small Animals, the Hospital for Large Animals, or the Tufts Wildlife Clinic.
- » Get up close and personal with the animals on the Cummings School Farm while learning proper animal handling techniques and performing physical examinations.

Description, Continued

- Build your vet skills! Practice bandaging and suturing, learn how to read x-rays, give a clinical exam to a dog, and work as a team to solve a challenging medical case.
- Participate in hematology and anatomy labs, meet various working dogs, visit a dairy farm, and more!
- Admission to the high school program is competitive.

Bard College at Simon's Rock Young Writers Workshop

Contact: Dr. Jamie Hutchinson, Director

Address: Young Writers Workshop
Bard College at Simon's Rock
84 Alford Rd.
Great Barrington, MA 01230

Phone: 413-528-7231

Fax: 413-528-7365

E-mail: jamieh@simons-rock.edu

Website: http://www.simons-rock.edu/young-writers

Program Type: Academic Enrichment

Grade/Age Levels: Rising grades 10–12

Description: The Young Writers Workshop was established at Simon's Rock in 1983 and is modeled after Bard College's innovative precollege writing program. Each year, 84 students are selected to participate. Unlike conventional workshops in creative or expository writing, Simon Rock's 3-week program focuses on using informal, playful expressive writing as a way to strengthen skills of language and thinking. Out of this informal writing, using techniques of peer response, students develop more polished pieces, from poems and stories, to reflective essays. Classes are small and emphasize an atmosphere of trust and collaboration. Emphasis is given to discovering one's personal voice as a writer. Students have the opportunity to attend plays, concerts, and other cultural activities that are part of summer life in the Berkshires.

BIMA at Brandeis University

Contact: Rabbi Charlie Schwartz

Address: BIMA
Brandeis University
415 South St.
MS 065
Waltham, MA 02454

Phone: 781-736-8416

Fax: 815-301-2874

E-mail: highschool@brandeis.edu

Website: http://www.brandeis.edu/highschool

Program Type: Academic Enrichment; Fine, Performing, and Visual Arts

Grade/Age Levels: Rising grades 9–12

Description: BIMA is Brandeis University's summer arts institute for high school students. We offer five core areas of artistic study: dance, music (choral, chamber, and jazz), theater, visual arts, and writing.

Our mission is to guide high school students as they develop their imaginative and artistic faculties to explore the relevance of Jewish tradition in their lives. BIMA is committed to the value of a serious and dynamic encounter between artistic expression and Jewish life. We aspire to serve as both a nurturing community and a creative catalyst for this interaction.

BIMA cultivates a vibrant, pluralistic environment for participants to hone their artistic skills, deepen their Jewish knowledge, and ask questions about their identity as young Jewish people committed to pursuing the arts.

BIMA connects young people from different backgrounds and different cultures—from across the nation and around the globe—who

Description, Continued

share a passion for the arts and Judaism. As you spend time with this dynamic group, you will explore the relationship between your Jewish identity and your artistic passions, all while living in Brandeis University dorms, getting a glimpse of college life, and building lifelong friendships.

BIMA is one of several programs, where passionate, motivated high school students immerse themselves in hands-on learning experiences while getting a taste of life on the Brandeis campus.

Boston Architectural College (BAC) High School Summer Academy

Address: Boston Architectural College
Continuing Education Department
320 Newbury St.
Boston, MA 02115

Phone: 617-585-0153

Fax: 617-585-0121

E-mail: summer@the-bac.edu

Website: http://www.the-bac.edu/summer

Program Type: Academic Enrichment

Grade/Age Levels: Grades 10 and up

Description: BAC Summer Academy is an exciting career exploration program for high school students who have a strong interest in architecture or design professions. Throughout the 4-week program, students experience the field of design through hands-on projects, interactive learning, and educational field trips. As part of their experience, students collaborate on a team venture to design and build a full-scale project. At the conclusion of the program, students' work will be exhibited at the BAC. Participants leave the program with new items for their portfolio and a stronger sense of whether to pursue a career in the field of design. Scholarships are available based on financial need, as well as through the Houseman/Kirkham Fund established to promote diversity in the design professions. Houseman Scholars attend BAC Summer Academy free of charge, may potentially be invited back the following summer to mentor new students, and will be eligible for a substantial scholarship to the Boston Architectural College to pursue a bachelor's degree in architecture, interior design, or landscape architecture.

Boston University Summer Term High School Programs

Contact:	Megan Hermida, Program Manager
Address:	Boston University Summer Term High School Programs 755 Commonwealth Ave., Room B05 Boston, MA 02215
Phone:	617-358-0646
Fax:	617-353-5532
E-mail:	summerhs@bu.edu
Website:	http://www.bu.edu/summer/high-school-programs
Program Type:	Academic Enrichment
Grade/Age Levels:	Grades 9–12
Description:	This summer, preview the college experience at one of the world's top teaching and research universities—in one of the most exciting U.S. cities. Boston University Summer Term offers five precollege summer programs that introduce you to college life and academics. You can enroll in BU undergraduate classes for college credit, pursue in-depth research in a university lab, or choose from an array of stimulating 1-, 2-, or 3-week noncredit seminars. Each of our high school programs provides you with an opportunity to explore new subjects while making friends with students from 49 states and 87 countries through fun social activities on campus and around Boston.

Boston University Summer Theatre Institute

Contact: Brian Dudley, Administrative Program Head

Address: Boston University Summer Theater Institute
College of Fine Arts
855 Commonwealth Ave., 4th Floor
Boston, MA 02215

Phone: 617-353-3390

Fax: 617-353-4363

E-mail: busti@bu.edu

Website: http://www.bu.edu/cfa/busti

Program Type: Fine, Performing, and Visual Arts

Grade/Age Levels: Grades 10–12

Description: The Boston University Summer Theatre Institute is an immersive 5-week program focused on performance training and theatre-making for highly motivated high school students. The program features coursework intended for the collaborative theatre-maker by offering a blend of performance, design, and production training. It is designed for those who wish to test their interests and abilities in a professional conservatory training environment. In this program, students develop confidence and technique, acquire insight and expertise, and learn to meet intellectual and artistic challenges. College credit is also available.

The Forsyth Institute Educational Outreach Program (EOP)

Contact: Dr. Martin Taubman, Program Director

Address: Educational Outreach Program
The Forsyth Institute
245 First Street
Cambridge, MA 02142

Phone: 617-262-5200

Fax: 617-262-4021

E-mail: mtaubman@forsyth.org

Website: http://forsyth.org/educational-outreach-program

Program Type: Internships/Paid Positions

Grade/Age Levels: Grades 9–11

Description: This summer program offers an 8-week paid internship for Boston public high school students, during which students are paired with Forsyth researchers as mentors. Over the summer, the interns learn basic laboratory techniques and participate in ongoing research projects. At the end of the program, students present scientific posters describing their findings. Students may continue working on their projects during the academic year. Student interns spend the summer in a productive and enriching environment. For these underrepresented youth, the Educational Outreach Program not only is often their first "real" job, but also may be their first step toward a future career path filled with challenges and achievements.

Non-Boston, nonpublic high school students may apply to the summer internship in an unpaid/volunteer position.

Genesis at Brandeis University

Contact: Rabbi Charlie Schwartz

Address: Genesis at Brandeis University
Brandeis University
415 South St.
MS 065
Waltham, MA 02454

Phone: 781-736-8416

Fax: 815-301-2874

E-mail: highschool@brandeis.edu

Website: http://www.brandeis.edu/highschool/genesis

Program Type: Academic Enrichment; Math, Sciences, Engineering, and Computer Science/ Technology

Grade/Age Levels: Rising grades 9–12

Description: Genesis is a one-month college experience program that brings together Jewish teens from around the world. At Genesis, you will be part of a dynamic community that shapes its own experiences through discussion, debate, Shabbat celebrations, and social action projects. Genesis participants learn from and teach one another, exchanging new ideas and practices, and forming lifelong friendships. You will also live and work with a team of educators who guide and inspire you in the challenging work of understanding diversity and creating community. Collaboration, discussion, and debate are welcomed, and your perspective will be heard and valued.

In addition to living in a dynamic residential environment at Brandeis University, you will take two main paths of study at Genesis. Participants choose a course, which will offer an in-depth, hands-on introduction to one of five academic disciplines: technology, gender and sexuality, entrepreneurship, science, or world religions. Participants collaborate to

Description, Continued

create options for the entire community to celebrate Shabbat. Genesis is supportive of all the ways in which Shabbat and Judaism are observed.

Every summer, Genesis brings together teens from different parts of the world, with varied interests and experiences of Judaism. We promise a learning experience like no other, a once-in-a-lifetime month of discoveries, insights, friendship, and fun.

Genesis is one of several programs where passionate, motivated high school students immerse themselves in hands-on learning experiences while getting a taste of life on the Brandeis campus.

Harvard: Project Success

Contact: Dr. Sheila Nutt, Director of Educational Outreach

Address: Office for Diversity Inclusion and Community Partnership
164 Longwood Ave., 2nd Floor
Boston, MA 02115

Phone: 617-432-4634

Fax: 617-432-3834

E-mail: sheila_nutt@hms.harvard.edu

Website: https://mfdp.med.harvard.edu/dicp-programs/k-12/high-school-programs/project-success

Program Type: Internships/Paid Positions

Grade/Age Levels: Grades 11–12

Description: Project Success is a rigorous academic summer program that targets students from under-represented groups and disadvantaged backgrounds who reside in Boston and Cambridge to participate in mentored summer research internships at Harvard Medical School and its affiliated institutions. The program is augmented by seminars and workshops given by faculty and administrators, site visits, and career guidance counseling. The program includes paid "hands-on" research positions for 8 weeks, from June through August, summer discussion series, seminars with researchers and physicians, site visits to hospitals and biotechnology firms, computer training, development of writing and speaking skills, academic year seminars and special programs, assigned mentors and research advisors, information about the college application process, and career counseling. Students must be 16 years of age by the first day of the program and possess a U.S. passport or other documentation giving permission to

Description, Continued work in America. Applications and brochures with additional eligibility requirements are only available upon request by e-mail: sheila_nutt@hms.harvard.edu.

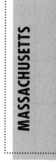

Harvard Secondary School Program

Contact: Mr. William Holinger, Director

Address: Harvard Secondary School Program
Harvard Summer School
51 Brattle St.
Cambridge, MA 02138

Phone: 617-495-3192

E-mail: ssp@dcemail.harvard.edu

Website: http://www.summer.harvard.edu/ssp

Program Type: Academic Enrichment

Grade/Age Levels: Rising grade 11 and up

Description: Students can choose from 200 courses offered at Harvard. They have a choice of 4-credit courses or one 8-credit course. Students will have access to a distinguished faculty, well-equipped labs, exceptional museums, and the largest university library system in the world. They will live and learn with students of many ages from all areas of the United States and more than 90 countries. Room and board is available. See website for details and course listing.

Harvard Summer School Pre-College Program

Contact: Ms. Jackie Newcomb

Address: Harvard Summer School
51 Brattle St.
Cambridge, MA 02138

Phone: 617-495-4024

E-mail: precollege@summer.harvard.edu

Website: http://www.summer.harvard.edu/programs/pre-college-program

Program Type: Academic Enrichment

Grade/Age Levels: Rising grades 11–12

Description: Immersive, collaborative, transformative—that's the Harvard Pre-College Program. Students take a 2-week noncredit course, exploring a topic in depth with Harvard faculty or visiting scholars. Subjects include law, computer science, writing, and philosophy. In this program, students become better critical thinkers and engaged citizens, focus on learning over achievement, and practice the art of healthy debate, delving into thought-provoking conversations and learning to embrace controversy diplomatically. Students also participate in college prep and social activities, live on campus, and enjoy a summer of discovery. See the website for details and course listing.

Mathcamp

Contact:	Marisa Debowsky, Program Director
Address:	Canada/USA Mathcamp 129 Hancock St. Cambridge, MA 02139
Phone:	888-371-4159
E-mail:	mc@mathcamp.org
Website:	http://www.mathcamp.org
Program Type:	Math, Sciences, Engineering, and Computer Science/Technology
Grade/Age Levels:	Ages 13–18
Description:	Canada/USA Mathcamp is an intensive 5-week-long summer program for mathematically talented high school students, designed to expose students to the beauty of advanced mathematical ideas and to new ways of thinking. More than just a summer camp, Mathcamp is a vibrant community, made up of a wide variety of people who share a common love of learning and passion for mathematics. At Mathcamp, students can explore undergraduate and even graduate-level topics while building problem-solving skills that will help them in any field they choose to study. The location varies each year; recent locations have included Portland, OR; Tacoma, WA; and Waterville, ME.

MIT Women's Technology Program

Contact: Ms. Cynthia Skier, Director

Address: Women's Technology Program
Massachusetts Institute of Technology
MIT Room 38-491
77 Massachusetts Ave.
Cambridge, MA 02139

Phone: 617-253-5580

E-mail: wtp@mit.edu

Website: http://wtp.mit.edu

Program Type: Math, Sciences, Engineering, and Computer Science/Technology

Grade/Age Levels: Grade 11

Description: The MIT Women's Technology Program (WTP) is a 4-week summer academic and residential experience where female high school students explore engineering and computer science through hands-on classes, labs, and team-based projects in their summer after 11th grade. Students attend WTP in either: Electrical Engineering and Computer Science (EECS) or Mechanical Engineering (ME). Courses are taught by female MIT graduate students. Students must apply by January 1 of their junior year to attend the following summer.

MASSACHUSETTS

Mock Trial Boot Camp

Contact: Joshua Mocle

Address: Mock Trial Boot Camp
Brandeis University
415 South St.
MS 065
Waltham, MA 02454

Phone: 781-736-8416

Fax: 815-301-2874

E-mail: highschool@brandeis.edu

Website: http://www.brandeis.edu/highschool/mocktrial

Program Type: Academic Enrichment

Grade/Age Levels: Rising grades 9–12

Description: Mock Trial Boot Camp gives students who are interested in law, public policy, and leadership an opportunity to gain knowledge and skills in legal analysis. Through a series of playful mini-trials, serious strategy sessions, and practical workshops, you will take your legal skills and understanding to a new level. Here's your chance to tackle the issues with world-class attorneys, judges, and law professors. Our final trial will be held in the Federal Courthouse in Boston.

Participants live in Brandeis University dorms and will visit sites of interest around Boston.

Mock Trial Boot Camp is one of several programs where passionate, motivated high school students immerse themselves in hands-on learning experiences while getting a taste of life on the Brandeis campus.

Program in Mathematics for Young Scientists (PROMYS)

Contact: Professor Glenn Stevens, Director

Address: The Program in Mathematics
for Young Scientists
Boston University
Department of Mathematics
111 Cummington Mall
Boston, MA 02215

Phone: 617-353-2563

Fax: 617-353-8100

E-mail: promys@math.bu.edu

Website: http://www.promys.org

Program Type: Math, Sciences, Engineering, and Computer Science/Technology

Grade/Age Levels: Grades 9–12

Description: PROMYS is a 6-week summer program at Boston University designed to encourage motivated high school students (grades 9–12, who are age 15 or older) to explore the creative world of mathematics in a supportive community of peers, counselors, research mathematicians, and visiting scientists.

Smith College Summer Science and Engineering Program

Contact: Dr. Sarah Craig

Address: Summer Science and Engineering Program
Smith College
Educational Outreach
Clark Hall
Northampton, MA 01063

Phone: 413-585-3060

Fax: 413-585-3068

E-mail: scraig@smith.edu

Website: http://www.smith.edu/summerprograms/ssep

Program Type: Math, Sciences, Engineering, and Computer Science/Technology

Grade/Age Levels: Rising grades 9–12

Description: This 4-week program is geared toward exceptional young women with strong interests in science, engineering, and medicine. Students take two 2-week science research courses of their choice, including lectures, field work, and science experiments. Financial aid is available.

New England School of Art & Design at Suffolk University Pre-College Program

Contact: Ms. Virginia Lane, Director of Continuing Education

Address: New England School of Art & Design
at Suffolk University
75 Arlington St.
Boston, MA 02116

Phone: 617-994-4233

Fax: 617-994-4250

E-mail: vlane@suffolk.edu

Website: http://www.suffolk.edu/pre_college

Program Type: Fine, Performing, and Visual Arts

Grade/Age Levels: Rising grades 10–13

Description: Pre-College is a fun and affordable way for high school sophomores, juniors, seniors, or entering college freshmen to study art and design at the college level and get connected with Boston's art and design scene. This 5-week summer program gives you a taste of the visual arts basics that all artists and designers must know—drawing, two- and three-dimensional design, and painting. We'll also explore some of the city's museums and galleries, and you'll get a chance to visit the studios of practicing artists and designers to see how they are making a living with their art.

Pre-College is more than just a great way to explore your creative interests. If you're thinking of studying art and design in college, we'll teach you how to prepare and present a portfolio for admission. And if you're entering

Description, Continued your senior year or are a recent grad who plans to come to Suffolk's School of Art & Design, the Pre-College Program can be used to waive the portfolio requirement for admissions to our Bachelor of Fine Arts programs in graphic design, illustration, interior design, and fine arts.

Summer at WPI

Address: WPI K–12 Summer Programs
Bartlett Center
100 Institute Rd.
Worcester, MA 01609

Phone: 508-831-4900

Fax: 508-831-5188

E-mail: summer@wpi.edu

Website: http://www.wpi.edu/+summer

Program Type: Math, Sciences, Engineering, and Computer Science/Technology; Academic Enrichment

Grade/Age Levels: Ages 7–18

Description: Summer at Worchester Polytechnic Institute is a chance for students to explore interests, challenge themselves, and try something new. Programs include day and overnight programs for kids ages 7–18; technology programs in robotics, computing, music, and more; science and leadership advancement for girls; sports camps for all ages; and expert instruction by WPI faculty and coaches.

Frontiers is a 2-week residential program in which students entering grades 11–12 are challenged to explore the outer limits of knowledge in science, technology, engineering, and mathematics (STEM). Students learn current laboratory techniques and explore unsolved problems across a wide spectrum of engineering and science disciplines.

Launch is a weeklong day or residential learning and research opportunity for students entering grades 9–10. Students choose one of the following fields: biology, chemistry/biochemistry, computer science, engineering technology, environmental modeling, interactive media and game design, intro to computer aided design (CAD), or robotics. Along with faculty, current WPI students, and classmates,

Description, Continued

students use state-of-the-art experimental, analytical, and computer technology to complete projects and assemble findings.

Leadership Academy for Young Women is for female students entering grades 8–10. Students develop leadership, presentation, and project management skills through fun activities such as mock political campaigns and performance art.

More program details and registration are available at http://www.wpi.edu/+summer.

Young Artist Residency Program

Contact: Lisa DeBenedictis, Program Manager

Address: College of Art and Design
Lesley University
29 Everett Street
Cambridge, MA 02138

Phone: 617-349-8011

E-mail: yar@lesley.edu

Website: http://www.lesley.edu/pre-college/young-artists-residency

Program Type: Fine, Performing, and Visual Arts; Academic Enrichment

Grade/Age Levels: Rising grades 11–12

Description: The Young Artist Residency Program at the Lesley University College of Art and Design is geared toward high school students who will be entering their junior or senior year in the fall. This intensive 4-week program is designed to offer a professional art college experience and open pathways to a career in art or design. Students enroll in a full schedule of visual art and design courses that they choose, study with college professors and graduates of the Lesley University College of Art and Design, and earn six college credits. Students also experience Cambridge, Boston, and a New England summer while living in residence halls on the Lesley University campus.

Acadia Institute of Oceanography (AIO)

Contact: Sheryl Gilmore, Executive Director

Address: Acadia Institute of Oceanography
P.O. Box 8308
Ann Arbor, MI 48107

Phone: 800-375-0058

E-mail: explore@acadiainstitute.com

Website: http://www.acadiainstitute.com

Program Type: Academic Enrichment

Grade/Age Levels: Ages 12–18

Description: AIO is a summer camp program for marine science studies based in Seal Harbor, ME. The unique program is designed for motivated young people between the ages of 12 and 18 who want to learn and have fun in the pristine ocean environment next to Acadia National Park. Sessions are coeducational. AIO offers basic and advanced sessions taught by professional staff. College credit is available for one advanced session each summer.

Summer Address (June 1 to Aug. 31):
Acadia Institute of Oceanography
P.O. Box 285
Seal Harbor, ME 04685
Phone: 207-276-9825

Interlochen Arts Camp

Contact: Sheryl Gilmore, Executive Director

Address: Interlochen Center for the Arts
Admissions Office
P.O. Box 199
Interlochen, MI 49643-0199

Phone: 800-681-5912

E-mail: admission@interlochen.org

Website: http://www.camp.interlochen.org

Program Type: Fine, Performing, and Visual Arts

Grade/Age Levels: Grades 3–12

Description: Each summer, more than 2,600 of the world's most talented and motivated young people come to Interlochen to live, learn, and perform with an unparalleled group of peers and educators. Founded in 1928, Interlochen is the first and foremost camp of its kind, offering both visual and performing arts camp programs for student artists in grades 3–12. This residential program provides study in creative writing, dance, general arts, motion picture arts, music, theatre arts, and visual arts.

MICHIGAN

Kettering University Pre-College Programs

Address: Kettering University
1700 W. University Ave., Room 3-100 CC
Flint, MI 48504-4898

Phone: 1-800-955-4464 ext. 7865

Website: http://www.kettering.edu/precollege

Program Type: Math, Sciences, Engineering, and Computer Science/Technology

Grade/Age Levels: Grades 6–12

Description: Kettering University's mission is to prepare students for lives of extraordinary leadership and service by linking transformative experiential learning opportunities to rigorous academic programs in science, technology, engineering, mathematics, and business. Kettering's precollege programs offer opportunities for students in junior high and high school, addressing a variety of topics and interests.

LITE is a 2-week residential program meant to introduce girls who will be entering grade 12 to what engineers do and how they improve people's lives by applying math, science, and technology to human problems. Participants will learn about everyday products that make a profound impact, such as air bags, artificial limbs, and car seats. Thirty-six selected participants from across the country will experience classes and labs taught by Kettering faculty in exciting subjects. For more information, contact Deborah Stewart, director, at LITE@kettering.edu.

Academically Interested Minds (AIM) is a 5-week, free, residential summer program designed to give multicultural students a real college life experience. Students attend

Description, Continued

freshman-level courses Monday–Thursday in calculus, chemistry, computer programming, economics, physics, and business management. Evenings and weekends include chaperoned activities. For more information, contact Ricky Brown, director, at rbrown@kettering.edu.

Computer Engineering Summer Day Camp is a one-week program for students in grades 9–12. Students design, build, and program a robot, exploring how robotic sensor technologies help make robots intelligent. Students also create and design their own Android smartphone application and use them to remotely control robots. For more information, contact Virginia Hill, program director, at vhill@kettering.edu.

For more programs, visit http://www.kettering.edu/precollege.

Michigan State University Engineering Summer Programs

Contact: Mr. Luis Donado, Recruiting and K–12 Outreach

Address: Michigan State University
College of Engineering
428 S. Shaw Lane, Room 3200
East Lansing, MI 48824

Phone: 517-353-7282

E-mail: donadoto@egr.msu.edu

Website: http://www.egr.msu.edu/future-engineer/programs

Program Type: Math, Sciences, Engineering, and Computer Science/Technology

Grade/Age Levels: Grades 4–12

Description: Introduction to Robotics Engineering at MSU is open to both U.S. and international students who are rising 10th–12th graders and is designed for those interested in exploring the exciting field of robotics. Students will learn about the fields of engineering involved in robotics and will work with NXT and VEX robotics, biomimetic robotic fish, nanorobotics, mechatronics and, manufacturing automation. The program focuses on short lectures, hands-on experiments, team work and lab tours. Presentations from different branches of MSU are also part of the program.

The High School Engineering Institute (HSEI) is intended for rising high school sophomores, juniors, and seniors seriously considering engineering as their career choice. This residential program is designed to give in-depth experiences in engineering majors. Each day, students will learn about a major and spend time with an engineering faculty

Description, Continued

member, a graduate student, or an undergraduate student engaged in short lecture, demonstrations, hands-on experiments, team-based problem solving, and tours. Presentations by the Honors College, Admissions Office, Study Abroad and The Center (Co-op/Internship and Undergraduate Research Opportunities), as well as tours of engineering research facilities, will be conducted.

Spartan Engineering for Teens is for rising eight and ninth graders dedicated to teaching future engineers and scientists the skills to be leaders in this exciting interdisciplinary field. Students in the program will use microsensors and robots while learning science, engineering, and mathematics. Working with science teachers and engineering faculty, students will design and build experiments. Students will learn about various engineering majors, and be involved in short courses, demonstrations, field trips, and hands-on experiments.

Visit the website for information about more programs, including those for fourth–eighth graders

Michigan Technological University Summer Youth Programs

Contact: Youth Programs Coordinator

Address: Michigan Tech Summer Youth Programs
217 Administration Bldg
1400 Townsend Dr.
Houghton, MI 49931-1295

Phone: 888-PRECOLLEGE

Fax: 906-487-1136

E-mail: syp@mtu.edu

Website: http://www.syp.mtu.edu

Program Type: Academic Enrichment

Grade/Age Levels: Grades 9–11

Description: The Michigan Technological University Summer Youth Programs (SYP) offer students an opportunity to experience a miniature version of college life. Scholarships are available.

Pre-College Explorations are for students who have completed grades 6–11 and possess an interest in discovery-based learning.

Women in Engineering (WIE) is for women who have completed grades 9, 10, or 11, and possess an interest in engineering.

Engineering Scholars Program (ESP) is for students who have completed grades 9, 10, or 11 and possess an interest in engineering.

National Summer Transportation Institute (NSTI) is for students who have completed grades 9, 10 or 11 and possess an interest in transportation fields.

Rail and Intermodal Transportation is for students who have completed grades 9, 10, or 11 and possess an interest in transportation fields.

Description, Continued

Women in Computer Science (WiCS) is for women who have completed grades 9, 10, or 11 and possess an interest in computer-based fields.

Yunasa (Michigan)

Contact: Yunasa Programs Coordinator

Address: Institute for Educational Advancement–Yunasa
569 S. Marengo Ave.
Pasadena, CA 91101

Phone: 626-403-8900

Fax: 626-403-8905

E-mail: yunasa@educationaladvancement.org

Website: http://www.educationaladvancement.org

Program Type: Leadership/Service/Volunteer

Grade/Age Levels: Ages 10–14

Description: The Institute for Educational Advancement (IEA) is an independent, national nonprofit that matches gifted children with customized educational programs designed to serve their complex intellectual and personal needs. Located in Fenton, MI, IEA's Yunasa is a week-long camp that unites highly able youngsters with experts in the social and emotional development of gifted children. In a nurturing setting, campers explore and grow the intellectual, spiritual, emotional, social, and physical aspects of their lives.

The camp offers guided imagery sessions, yoga, and traditional camp activities, as well as a wide variety of workshops focusing on topics such as teambuilding, leadership skills, and character building. The emphasis of all activities is on achieving balance, reminding campers that they are more than just intellect.

Every camper will learn techniques for integrating all aspects of their lives through small-group workshops led by Yunasa's esteemed faculty. These experts have years of experience working with gifted youth and shaping gifted discourse in the U.S. through

Description, Continued education, curriculum development, psychology practice, research, and writing.

Yunasa offers campers an opportunity to build community with like-minded peers, escape their busy everyday schedules, challenge themselves to develop into their personal best, gain self-acceptance, make lifelong friends, and have fun!

Carleton Liberal Arts Experience (CLAE)

MINNESOTA

Contact: Mr. Brian Swann, Director of Outreach Programs

Address: Carleton College
100 S. College St.
Northfield, MN 55057

Phone: 800-995-2275

Fax: 507-222-4526

E-mail: clae@carleton.edu

Website: http://go.carleton.edu/clae

Program Type: Academic Enrichment

Grade/Age Levels: Rising grade 11

Description: The Carleton Liberal Arts Experience (CLAE) will select 50 high school students who are current sophomores and bring them to Carleton College, all expenses paid, for a one-week summer program. Students of African American descent or students who have an interest in African American culture are encouraged to apply. The CLAE program introduces the strengths of a liberal arts education through an array of courses in science, art, social sciences, and technology. Students should have finished their sophomore year prior to the summer of the program. Past course offerings include DNA Analysis: The Science of Forensics, Write Your Way In: Strategies for Success on Your College Application, Motown and American Culture, Religion and the Black Freedom Struggle, and The Ordovician Ocean.

Carleton College Summer Computer Science Institute (SCSI)

Address: Summer Academic Programs
Summer Computer Science Institute
Carleton College
One North College St.
Northfield, MN 55057

Phone: 507-222-4038; 866-767-2275 (toll-free)

Fax: 507-222-4540

E-mail: scsi@carleton.edu

Website: http://go.carleton.edu/scsi

Program Type: Math, Sciences, Engineering, and Computer Science/Technology

Grade/Age Levels: Rising grades 11 and 12

Description: The Summer Computer Science Institute (SCSI) focuses on understanding how to think about the processes for solving problems, how to program computers to implement them, and how to apply computer science ideas to real problems of interest. Students at SCSI will learn how to systematically approach problems like a computer scientist as they engage in classroom learning, hands-on lab activities, and collaborative, guided research directed by Carleton faculty and mentored by undergraduate research assistants. The program will culminate with the SCSI Research Symposium, where students will demonstrate the results of their guided research project.

Carleton College Summer Quantitative Reasoning Institute (SQRI)

MINNESOTA

Address: Summer Academic Programs
Summer Quantitative Reasoning Institute
Carleton College
One North College St.
Northfield, MN 55057

Phone: 507-222-4038; 866-767-2275 (toll-free)

Fax: 507-222-4540

E-mail: sqri@carleton.edu

Website: http://go.carleton.edu/sqri

Program Type: Academic Enrichment

Grade/Age Levels: Rising grades 11 and 12

Description: The Summer Quantitative Reasoning Institute (SQRI) focuses on how to use quantitative data to support one's arguments and evaluate those of others. The Institute is not a "math camp," but an intense program of training in several social science disciplines: political science and international relations, economics, and psychology. Students will learn how to think like a social scientist by not only receiving instruction in how these disciplines study the world, but by designing and engaging in a sustained, 3-week collaborative research project with peers and their faculty mentors. Students will be trained in how to use the statistical tools of these disciplines to answer a variety of research questions.

Carleton Summer Science Institute (CSSI)

Address: Summer Academic Programs
Carleton Summer Science Institute
Carleton College
One North College St.
Northfield, MN 55057

Phone: 507-222-4038; 866-767-2275 (toll-free)

Fax: 507-222-4540

E-mail: cssi@carleton.edu

Website: http://go.carleton.edu/cssi

Program Type: Math, Sciences, Engineering, and Computer Science/Technology

Grade/Age Levels: Rising grades 10 and 11

Description: The Carleton Summer Science Institute (CSSI) will help students learn to think and write like a scientist by doing science. CSSI students, faculty, and Carleton undergraduate research assistants will engage in classroom hands-on research related to faculty and student interests. Students will complete a collaborative, guided research project that will culminate in a presentation at the CSSI Research Symposium held at the end of the program.

Carleton College Summer Writing Program

MINNESOTA

Address: Summer Academic Programs
Summer Writing Program
Carleton College
One North College St.
Northfield, MN 55057

Phone: 507-222-4038; 866-767-2275 (toll-free)

Fax: 507-222-4540

E-mail: swp@carleton.edu

Website: http://go.carleton.edu/swp

Program Type: Academic Enrichment

Grade/Age Levels: Rising grade 11

Description: Every summer, more than 60 high school sophomores and juniors gather on the campus of Carleton College for 3 weeks of intensive writing instruction, fun, and friendship. Emphasizing a writing process approach, this program helps students learn to compose academic papers that are similar to those they will write in college. Students read both contemporary and traditional literature, which then become the focus of their essays. The program is for college-bound students in their sophomore or junior year of high school.

Carleton College Summer Humanities Institute

Address: Summer Academic Programs
Summer Humanities Institute
Carleton College
One North College St.
Northfield, MN 55057

Phone: 507-222-4038; 866-767-2275 (toll-free)

Fax: 507-222-4540

E-mail: shi@carleton.edu

Website: http://go.carleton.edu/shi

Program Type: Academic Enrichment

Grade/Age Levels: Rising grades 11–12

Description: Guided by professors in history, English literature, and art history, the Summer Humanities Institute (SHI) participants will look at ways in which humanists discovered and interpreted ancient texts, employing them as sources of cultural power and tools to build and shape their society. Participants will examine how artists working in Rome, like Michelangelo and Caravaggio, combined elements of classical aesthetics and contemporary sensibilities to develop new modes of visual story-telling and emotional expression. Over 3 weeks, participants will develop and present interdisciplinary, guided research projects in history, English literature, or art history, and will acquire and learn to effectively use tools and techniques of research, interpretations, and presentation essential to achieve the goal of humanistic research: to understand with depth and complexity the nature of human thought, action, and expression.

Carleton College Summer Language and Global Issues Institute

MINNESOTA

Address: Summer Academic Programs
Language and Global Issues Summer Institute
Carleton College
One North College St.
Northfield, MN 55057

Phone: 507-222-4038; 866-767-2275 (toll-free)

Fax: 507-222-4540

E-mail: lgi@carleton.edu

Website: http://go.carleton.edu/lgii

Program Type: Academic Enrichment; Foreign Language

Grade/Age Levels: Rising grades 11–12

Description: The Summer Language and Global Issues Institute is a unique opportunity for intensive language instruction combined with an introduction to global topics. Students who participate in LGI will spend several hours each day totally immersed in French or Spanish, both in class and in extracurricular activities. Students will improve language skills, benefitting from formal instruction while using foreign language to communicate about important topics. Students sign a language pledge to use only their foreign language during the first half of each day. Afternoon coursework (taught in English) will focus on issues of immigration in various regions of the world, introducing students to the multiple disciplines (history, religion, literature, economics, sociology, political science, etc.) needed to understand such a complex topic.

Concordia Language Villages

Address:	Concordia College Concordia Language Villages 901 8th St. S. Moorhead, MN 56562
Phone:	800-222-4750
Fax:	218-299-3807
E-mail:	clv@cord.edu
Website:	http://www.concordialanguagevillages.org
Program Type:	Foreign Language
Grade/Age Levels:	Ages 7–18
Description:	Concordia Language Villages offers multiple language programs in Arabic, Chinese, Danish, English, Finnish, French, German, Italian, Japanese, Korean, Norwegian, Portuguese, Russian, Spanish, and Swedish. Students can choose from one-week explorations, 2-week immersions, 4-week high school or college credit programs, and various wilderness, science, and adventure programs.

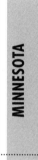

Summer College for High School Students

Address: Summer College for High School Students
12-B E.F. Yerby Conference Center
689 Grove Loop
The University of Mississippi
University, MS 38677

Phone: 662-915-7621

Fax: 662-915-5138

E-mail: summercollege@olemiss.edu

Website: http://www.outreach.olemiss.edu/schs/index.html

Program Type: Academic Enrichment; Math, Sciences, Engineering, and Computer Science/Technology; Fine, Performing, and Visual Arts

Grade/Age Levels: Grades 11–12

Description: Summer College for High School Students offers academically gifted juniors and seniors the opportunity to study in specialized programs, take top-notch academic courses for college credit, and get a real glimpse at what life on a college campus is like. Potential areas of study include computer science, engineering, health professions, Integrated Marketing Communications, English, Spanish, journalism, legal studies, and theatre.

University of Mississippi Summer Academy

Address: Pre-College Programs, Summer Academy
P.O. Box 1848
The University of Mississippi
University, MS 38677-0009

Phone: 662-915-7621

Website: http://www.outreach.olemiss.edu/youth/summer_academy/index.html#why

Program Type: Academic Enrichment; Math, Sciences, Engineering, and Computer Science/Technology; Fine, Performing, and Visual Arts

Grade/Age Levels: Grades 8–10

Description: The University of Mississippi's Summer Academy gives students entering the 8th–10th grades a taste of college life. Through the Summer Academy, students make new friends and contacts, learn time management, improve study habits, and earn high school credit that can count toward high school graduation requirements.

Depending on grade level and term selected, students will explore the world's cultures, flex their imaginations, learn about human behavior, investigate Earth's delicate balances, conduct science experiments, or publish a literary magazine. Past course offerings have included astronomy, botany, creative writing, public speaking, mythology, environmental science, fantasy fiction, and personal finance.

The University of Southern Mississippi Summer Programs

Address: The University of Southern Mississippi
The Frances A. Karnes Center for
Gifted Studies
118 College Dr. #5123
Hattiesburg, MS 39406-0001

Phone: 601-266-5236

Fax: 601-266-4764

E-mail: gifted.studies@usm.edu

Website: http://www.usm.edu/gifted

Program Type: Leadership/Service/Volunteer; Academic Enrichment

Grade/Age Levels: Grades 6–11

Description: The Leadership Studies Program is a one-week residential program for students in grades 6–11 who desire to develop and enhance their leadership ability. Leadership I includes the fundamentals necessary for leadership development. Leadership II (prerequisite Leadership I) is a continuation of leadership concepts and qualities. Leadership III (prerequisite Leadership II) focuses on the legal aspects and responsibilities of leadership positions.

The Summer Program for Academically Talented Youth is a 3-week residential program for students in grades 7–10 who qualify based on SAT or ACT results. A variety of intensive, fast-paced courses are offered, such as precalculus mathematics; human anatomy/physiology; forensic science; polymer science; criminal justice; psychology; creative writing; debate; and political science. The program is designed to include appropriate academic,

Description, Continued cultural, and recreational experiences. The University of Southern Mississippi offers the program through cooperative efforts with the Duke University Talent Identification Program.

Cub Creek Science and Animal Camp

Contact: Ms. Lori Martin, Director

Address: Cub Creek Science and Animal Camp
16795 State Rt. E
Rolla, MO 65401

Phone: 573-458-2125

Fax: 573-458-2126

E-mail: Director@BearRiverRanch.com

Website: http://mosciencecamp.com

Program Type: Academic Enrichment

Grade/Age Levels: Ages 7–17

Description: A residential summer camp offering one-to 6-week sessions, Cub Creek Science and Animal Camp offers the ultimate experience for the animal enthusiast. The camp is home to more than 200 animals from more than 100 different species and it offers one of the only Junior Vet programs in the country. Cub Creek Science Camp combines learning with good old-fashioned fun. Cub Creek is a place where kids can splash in the pool, explore a mud cave, roast marshmallows over a campfire, and make lifelong friends all while learning about science and animals. Campers attend Cub Creek from nearly every state and many other countries.

Joseph Baldwin Academy for Eminent Young Scholars

Address: Joseph Baldwin Academy
for Eminent Young Scholars
Truman State University
100 East Normal
Baldwin Hall 110
Kirksville, MO 63501

Phone: 660-785-5406

Fax: 660-785-7202

E-mail: jmorton@truman.edu

Website: http://jba.truman.edu

Program Type: Academic Enrichment

Grade/Age Levels: Rising grades 8–10

Description: The Joseph Baldwin Academy offers students (rising grades 8–10) the opportunity to engage in an intensive 3-week residential program with an academically challenging curriculum. Students enroll in one concentrated college course, which meets 6 hours each weekday and 3 hours on Saturdays. Classes are taught by university faculty. The curriculum has included the following courses, among others: Advocacy, Argument, and Persuasion: Classical Rhetoric in Contemporary Times; Adventures in Pop Culture Studies; Can You Say That With Your Hands? An Introduction to American Sign Language and Deaf Culture; Computers in Art and Design; Introduction to Chemistry; Psychology Through Science Fiction; The Beauty of Mathematics: Elementary Problems in Quantity, Structure, and Space; The Horse: Equine History, Biology, and Riding; The Human Laboratory; Theater: Onstage and Off; Writing Nature; An "Animated" Course; Ancient Greek: A

Description, Continued

Modern Odyssey; Biomusicology: The Study of Music from a Biological Perspective; Creating a Useable Past: Genealogy and Local History; Preparatory College Mathematics; Journalism; The Art and Science of Computer Programming; The Writer's Craft; Why We Fought: American Wars From World War I to Iraq; World Mythology: Myths, Mythemes, and Making Meaning; and Drawing. New courses are added each year. The Joseph Baldwin Academy is proud to provide an academic challenge to younger students that is truly one of the finest, and most affordable, of such opportunities in the nation.

Summer Talent Academy for Professions in Health

Address: Summer Talent Academy
for Professions in Health
Truman State University
100 East Normal
Baldwin Hall 110
Kirksville, MO 63501

Phone: 660-785-5406

Fax: 660-785-7202

E-mail: jmorton@truman.edu

Website: http://staph.truman.edu

Program Type: Academic Enrichment

Grade/Age Levels: Rising grades 11–12

Description: The Summer Talent Academy for Professions in Health (STAPH) offers highly talented students interested in science and health a one-week residential opportunity to explore medicine and allied health professions. Students live as college students while exploring the work of medical professionals. Most importantly, they work with highly regarded faculty and health professionals from Truman State University and A.T. Still University of Health Sciences—home of the very first college of Osteopathic Medicine.

We believe that many rising high school juniors and seniors will benefit from this intensive experience challenging them academically and stimulating their interest in health professions. The primary goal of STAPH is that our students leave with an increased appreciation for the excitement of learning, increased engagement with topics in health, and a meaningful sampling of the college experience. Along the way, we expect

Description, Continued that they will grow both academically and socially as they interact with other high-ability students from across the country and that they will develop a new enthusiasm for careers in health.

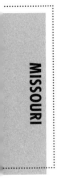

Zombie Scholars Academy: A Problem-Based Exploration of Science, Literature, and Leadership

Address: Zombie Scholars Academy
Truman State University
100 East Normal
Baldwin Hall 110
Kirksville, MO 63501

Phone: 660-785-5406

Fax: 660-785-7202

E-mail: jmorton@truman.edu

Website: http://zombie.truman.edu

Program Type: Academic Enrichment

Grade/Age Levels: Rising grades 9–12

Description: The Zombie Scholars Academy is a summer learning experience like you've never seen before! And if you think the title tells you everything you need to know—think again! ZSA is a unique academic program that takes the unprecedented interest young people have in the thrilling—and often humorous—fiction of a zombie apocalypse and turns that energy into a fantastic vehicle for learning about some of society's most pressing needs.

Why do we enjoy dystopian novels and movies like *The Hunger Games*, *V for Vendetta*, *Total Recall*, *Fahrenheit 451*, or *The Planet of the Apes*? Why do plot lines about romances between humans and vampires or werewolves attract so many to the box office? Why do scenarios about the end of the world or organized society make for some of the most popular offerings on TV? Aside from the purely thrilling or humorous elements of these plots, we believe the fundamental reason why

Description, Continued

people—particularly young people—love these stories so much is that they provoke creative thought about REAL problems we face. These stories ask us to imagine what we would do in a crisis, what science would do to help us, and how we'd solve problems without the benefit of resources we take for granted. In short, these stories turn on that part of our brain that makes us think most critically. Because the subject matter is fictional, we can enjoy that creative experience that much more.

The Zombie Scholars Academy takes this idea and turns it into a dynamic one-week residential summer learning experience, exposing students to great opportunities in biology, mathematics, creative writing, social science, group leadership, and problem solving.

Students and Teachers As Research Scientists (STARS)

Contact: Dr. Kenneth Mares, Director

Address: Students and Teachers As Research Scientists
University of Missouri-St. Louis
Department of Biology
239 Research Building
One University Blvd.
St. Louis, MO 63121-4400

Phone: 314-516-6155

Fax: 314-516-6233

E-mail: maresk@umsl.edu

Website: http://www.umsl.edu/~sep/STARS

Program Type: Academic Enrichment

Grade/Age Levels: Rising grade 12

Description: Eighty high potential secondary school students (rising seniors) have the opportunity to participate in research projects in anthropology, astronomy, biology, chemistry, computer science, engineering, mathematics, physics, or psychology at one of these collaborating research institutions: Saint Louis University, Washington University, University of Missouri-St. Louis, or Donald Danforth Plant Science Center. During this 6-week summer program, students do research within a community of investigators under the supervision of a practicing research mentor and present their findings in a research paper at the end of the program, which includes an oral presentation of their findings in a seminar format.

All Girls/All Math Summer Camp for High School Girls

Address: All Girls/All Math Summer Camp
for High School Girls
University of Nebraska-Lincoln
Center for Science, Math, and
Computer Education
251 Avery Hall
Lincoln, NE 68588-0131

Phone: 402-472-8965

Fax: 402-472-9311

E-mail: agam@unl.edu

Website: http://www.math.unl.edu/programs/agam

Program Type: Academic Enrichment

Grade/Age Levels: Grades 10–12

Description: All Girls/All Math Summer Camp for high school girls at the University of Nebraska-Lincoln provides a stimulating and supportive environment for girls to develop their mathematical ability and interest. Camp participants take a weeklong course about mathematical codes, as well as mini-courses on topics such as bioinformatics, aerodynamics, and knots. The girls will work with female mathematics professors and graduate students, and interact with peers who share an interest in mathematics. Candidates must be entering grades 10–12 year and must have successfully completed high school geometry.

THINK Summer Institute

Contact: Summer Programs Coordinator

Address: Davidson Institute for Talent Development
9665 Gateway Dr., Ste. B
Reno, NV 89521

Phone: 775-852-3483 ext. 438

Fax: 775-852-2184

E-mail: THINK@DavidsonGifted.org

Website: http://www.davidsongifted.org/think

Program Type: Academic Enrichment

Grade/Age Levels: Ages 13–16

Description: Gifted students interested in a challenging academic summer program should consider attending the THINK Summer Institute on the campus of the University of Nevada, Reno. This intense 3-week residential summer program offers exceptionally gifted 13–16-year-old students the opportunity to earn up to six transferable college credits.

Windsor Mountain International Summer Camp

Contact: Jake Labovitz, Director

Address: One World Way
Windsor, NH 03244

Phone: 800-862-7760

Fax: 603-478-5260

E-mail: jake@windsormountain.org

Website: http://www.windsormountain.org

Program Type: Academic Enrichment; Fine, Performing, and Visual Arts

Grade/Age Levels: Ages 7–16

Description: Windsor Mountain International Summer Camp, formerly Interlocken International Summer Camp, is a top-rated, private, traditional summer camp. This noncompetitive, overnight, coed camp in southwest New Hampshire provides 2-week and 3-week sessions. The free-choice program encourages campers to try new things, and the warm and diverse international camp community makes people feel at home. Specialty programs include New England sailing camp, film camp, performing arts camp, and visual arts camp, as well as 3-day wilderness adventure trips.

Appel Farm Arts Camp

Contact: Cori Solomon, Executive Director

Address: Appel Farm Arts Camp
457 Shirley Rd.
P.O. Box 888
Elmer, NJ 08318

Phone: 856-358-2472

Fax: 856-358-6513

E-mail: camp@appelfarm.org

Website: http://www.appelfarmartscamp.org

Program Type: Fine, Performing, and Visual Arts

Grade/Age Levels: Ages 7–17

Description: Appel Farm is a coeducational residential camp with programs in music, theater, dance, visual arts, photography, video, recording arts, creative writing, sports, and swimming. Appel Farm's camp combines arts classes with outdoor activities and community service on its 176-acre property in New Jersey. The student/teacher ratio for courses is 3:1.

Coriell Institute for Medical Research Summer Experience for Students

Address: Coriell Institute
Summer Experience Program—HR
403 Haddon Ave.
Camden, NJ 08103

Phone: 856-966-7377

Fax: 856-964-0254

E-mail: summerexperience@coriell.org

Website: https://www.coriell.org/education/summer-experience

Program Type: Math, Sciences, Engineering, and Computer Science/Technology

Grade/Age Levels: Ages 17 and up

Description: Coriell Institute invites a limited number of motivated students to participate in a Summer Experience program to gain insight into the workings of a renowned research institute. The 4-week internship-like program typically runs during the month of July, 4 days a week from 9 a.m. to 2 p.m. Student interns, who are at least 17 years of age, rotate through various laboratories and departments, including Cell Culture, Molecular Biology, Cytogenics, Biobanking, and Communications and Development.

Rutgers Young Scholars Program in Discrete Mathematics

Contact: Ms. Jean Mara

Address: Rutgers Young Scholars Program
DIMACS—CORE Building
96 Frelinghuysen Road
Piscataway, NJ 08854

Phone: 848-445-4065

Fax: 848-445-2894

E-mail: jemara@dimacs.rutgers.edu

Website: http://www.dimacs.rutgers.edu/ysp

Program Type: Math, Sciences, Engineering, and Computer Science/Technology

Grade/Age Levels: Grades 9–11

Description: The Rutgers Young Scholars Program in Discrete Mathematics is designed to encourage talented students, grades 9–11, to consider careers in the mathematical sciences. Selected students participate in an intensive 4-week residential academic program that provides a challenging introduction to discrete mathematics, a new and growing area of the mathematical sciences with many applications on the cutting edge of modern research.

Summer Science Program

Contact: Mr. Richard Bowdon, Executive Director

Address: Summer Science Program
108 Whiteberry Dr.
Cary, NC 27519

Phone: 866-728-0999

Fax: 954-862-3051

E-mail: info@summerscience.org

Website: http://www.summerscience.org

Program Type: Math, Sciences, Engineering, and Computer Science/Technology

Grade/Age Levels: Rising grades 11 and 12

Description: One of the longest running and most successful precollege enrichment programs, SSP offers motivated students an exciting immersion into real-world, hands-on science. Working in teams of three, students perform an astronomical research project from start to finish: They determine the orbit of an asteroid from their own observations, measurements, and software. College-level lectures in astronomy, physics, calculus, and programming provide the practical and theoretical tools for each student to understand what he or she is doing and why. Although the pace is challenging, the emphasis is on cooperation, not competition. This 6-week residential program includes behind-the-scenes field trips to places like the Very Large Array. SSP takes place at two campuses: New Mexico Tech in Socorro, NM, and The University of Colorado in Boulder. The curriculum is identical at each.

University of New Mexico Youth Programs

Address: University of New Mexico
Continuing Education
1634 University Blvd. NE
Albuquerque, NM 87131-4006

Phone: 505-277-0077

Fax: 505-277-1990

E-mail: ceregistration@unm.edu

Website: http://ce.unm.edu/youth

Program Type: Academic Enrichment

Grade/Age Levels: Ages 6–17

Description: The University of New Mexico Youth Program is dedicated to launching a lifetime love of learning in the youth we serve. Through partnerships with UNM departments, educational organizations, and other universities, we offer classes and camps designed to engage children and teens in enriching and challenging experiences taught by expert instructors that encourage creativity, develop talents and skills, and support the overall goals of each participant. We offer teens the opportunity to learn job skills and explore career paths through hands-on camps across the disciplines. Previous course offerings have included babysitting safety certification, yoga, tae kwon do, theatre, jewelry-making, and introductory classes in law, architecture, engineering, sustainability, and writing.

Alfred University Summer Programs for High School Students

Contact: Ms. Bonnie Dungan, Director of Summer Programs

Address: Alfred University Summer Programs for High School Students
Carnegie Hall
1 Saxon Dr.
Alfred, NY 14802

Phone: 607-871-2612

Fax: 607-871-2045

E-mail: summerpro@alfred.edu; dunganbj@alfred.edu

Website: http://www.alfred.edu/summer/camps

Program Type: Academic Enrichment

Grade/Age Levels: Grades 10–12

Description: Alfred University's summer programs invite high school students on campus to learn more about their fields of interest, sample college life, and meet other students with similar interests. The university offers summer institutes and camps in:

» Astronomy
» Art Portfolio Prep
» Chemistry
» Computer Engineering
» Creative Writing
» Ceramic Engineering
» Equestrian
» Robotics
» Renewable Energy Engineering
» Swimming
» Theater

NEW YORK

Boyce Thompson Institute for Plant Research (BTI) Internships

Address: Boyce Thompson Institute for Plant Research
533 Tower Road
Ithaca, NY 14853-1801

Phone: 607-254-6732

E-mail: pgrp-outreach@cornell.edu

Website: http://bti.cornell.edu/education/internships

Program Type: Internships/Paid Positions

Grade/Age Levels: Ages 16 and up

Description: The Boyce Thompson Institute for Plant Research at Cornell University offers summer internships to enrolled undergraduate and high school students interested in biological research. The internships provide an opportunity to gain research experience and explore scientific careers. Current opportunities are in two areas: plant genome research and bioinformatics.

Students in the Plant Genome Research Program (PGRP) summer internship program learn how basic plant research can be applied to the environment, enhance human health, and improve agriculture. PGRP interns gain knowledge of plant genomics and scientific research by working closely with scientists, postdoctoral fellows, and graduate students in a laboratory setting.

Bioinformatics interns will focus on developing computational tools and resources to store, analyze, and integrate large-scale plant "omics" datasets. The program offers a unique interdisciplinary training in plant genome research, computer programming, and systems biology. Students should have some prior experience with computer programming, biology, bioinformatics, and a demonstrated interest in the subject.

Description, Continued

Local high school students who are at least 16 years of age at the start of the program are eligible to apply. Housing is not provided and students must provide their own transportation to and from BTI each day. High school students receive stipends but are not provided with housing, travel, or meal allowances.

Cooper Union Summer STEM Program

Contact: George J. Delagrammatikas, Director

Address: Summer Research Internship Program
The Cooper Union
Albert Nerken School of Engineering
41 Cooper Square
New York, NY 10003

Phone: 212-353-4286

Fax: 212-353-4341

E-mail: summerstem@cooper.edu

Website: http://summer-stem.cooper.edu

Program Type: Math, Sciences, Engineering, and Computer Science/Technology

Grade/Age Levels: Grades 10–11

Description: The Summer STEM Program is an intensive, 6-week experience that immerses students in hands-on engineering design and problem solving, thereby placing them on the right track for careers in technological innovation. Students work closely with Cooper Union faculty and associated instructors at the forefront of engineering education.

Projects range broadly and include robotics, digital fabrication, computer programming and app development, biomedical and genetic engineering, improved urban infrastructure, and even racecar design. Faculty and teaching assistants from the departments of civil, chemical, electrical, and mechanical engineering provide students with foundational knowledge and expert guidance to address real-world problems in their respective disciplines of expertise.

Cornell Association for the Technological Advancement of Learned Youth in Science and Technology (CATALYST) Academy

NEW YORK

Address: CATALYST Academy
Diversity Programs in Engineering
Cornell University
146 Olin Hall
Ithaca, NY 14853

Phone: 607-255-6403

Fax: 607-255-2834

E-mail: dpeng@cornell.edu

Website: http://www.engineering.cornell.edu/catalyst

Program Type: Math, Sciences, Engineering, and Computer Science/Technology; Academic Enrichment

Grade/Age Levels: Rising grade 10 and up

Description: The CATALYST Academy is a one-week summer residential program for rising high school sophomores, juniors, and seniors. The mission of the CATALYST Academy is to advance diversity in engineering and its related disciplines. Therefore, applications from students from backgrounds (African American, Latino/a, or Native American) critically underrepresented in the fields of science, technology, engineering, and math are especially encouraged.

This summer, spend a week making new friends, experience life on a university campus, and explore the many exciting possibilities awaiting you in engineering!

Description, Continued

During the CATALYST Academy, Cornell University's world-renowned faculty and graduate students lead participants in classes, lab sessions, and project research. Social events, panel discussions, and other out-of-classroom activities provide participants with opportunities to network informally with Cornell faculty, staff, and students.

Cornell University Summer College Programs for High School Students

Address: Cornell University Summer College
B20 Day Hall
Ithaca, NY 14853-2801

Phone: 607-255-6203

Fax: 607-255-6665

E-mail: summer_college@cornell.edu

Website: http://www.summercollege.cornell.edu

Program Type: Academic Enrichment

Grade/Age Levels: Grades 10–12

Description: Cornell University Summer College offers 3- and 6-week programs for talented high school sophomores, juniors, and seniors. Students take college classes with leading Cornell faculty, earn an average of three to six credits, explore careers and academic majors, enjoy social and cultural activities, and attend admissions workshops. Students select a program from one of the following subjects: animal science, architecture, art, business, college success, debate and rhetoric, design, engineering, English language, environmental studies, fashion, history, hotel management, humanities, law and government, leadership, medicine, politics, psychology, research and science, social entrepreneurship, and veterinary medicine.

The CURIE Academy

Address: The Curie Academy
Diversity Programs in Engineering
Cornell University
146 Olin Hall
Ithaca, NY 14853

Phone: 607-255-6403

Fax: 607-255-2834

E-mail: dpeng@cornell.edu

Website: http://www.engineering.cornell.edu/curie

Program Type: Math, Sciences, Engineering, and Computer Science/Technology; Academic Enrichment

Grade/Age Levels: Rising grades 11–12

Description: The CURIE Academy is a one-week summer residential program for high school girls who excel in math and science The focus is on juniors and seniors who may not have had prior opportunities to explore engineering, but want to learn more about the many opportunities in engineering in an interactive atmosphere.

Cornell University's world-renowned faculty and graduate students will lead CURIE participants in classes, lab sessions, and project research. Social events, panel discussions, and other out-of-classroom activities will provide participants with opportunities to network informally with Cornell faculty, staff, and students.

Join us for the CURIE Academy and spend a week making new friends, experiencing life on a university campus, and exploring the many exciting possibilities awaiting you in engineering!

Environmental Studies Summer Youth Institute (ESSYI)

NEW YORK

Contact: Professor Jim MaKinster, Director

Address: Environmental Studies Summer
Youth Institute
300 Pulteney St.
Geneva, NY 14456

Phone: 315-781-4401

Fax: 315-781-3843

E-mail: essyi@hws.edu

Website: http://essyi.hws.edu

Program Type: Academic Enrichment

Grade/Age Levels: Ages 16–18

Description: The institute offers a 2-week, college-level interdisciplinary program for talented high school students entering their junior and senior years.

Students will conduct research with Hobart and William Smith faculty members in a variety of locations: on the *HWS William F. Scandling* (a 65-foot vessel on Seneca Lake), and in streams, quaking bogs, the Adirondack Mountains, and the college science laboratories.

Working in the field, in laboratories, in classrooms, and on a 4-day camping trip, students explore a range of topics in environmental policy, economics, and ethics, and come to see the natural world through the eyes of artists, historians, philosophers, and scientists.

Hofstra University Summer Science Research Program (HUSSRP)

Contact: Ms. Gail K. Bennington, Director

Address: Hofstra Summer Science Research Program
Gittleson Hall, Room 140
Hofstra University
Hempstead, NY 11549-1510

Phone: 516-463-4795

Fax: 516-463-5120

E-mail: gail.k.bennington@hofstra.edu

Website: http://www.hofstra.edu/Academics/Colleges/HCLAS/SSE

Program Type: Math, Sciences, Engineering, and Computer Science/Technology

Grade/Age Levels: Rising grades 11–12

Description: Hofstra University's Summer Science Research Program offers high school students opportunities in science research under the guidance of professionals in science and mathematics. For more than 10 years, HUSSRP has provided selected research-oriented high school students the opportunity to work with our science faculty during the summer in an on-campus research program. The nonresidential 6-week program begins in early July and runs through mid-August, culminating in a science "poster session" in September where students display the work they performed during the summer. The poster session is open to all students in the program and gives them the opportunity to present their research to science professionals and their peers in a noncompetitive environment. Students are selected for Hofstra's program on the basis of their high school science experience, research interests, a personal interview, and, above all, a high school teacher's recommendation.

Link Summer STEM Explorations

Address: Link Summer STEM Explorations
Kopernik Observatory & Science Center
698 Underwood Rd.
Vestal, NY 13850

Phone: 607-748-3685

E-mail: info@kopernik.org

Website: http://www.kopernik.org/

Program Type: Math, Sciences, Engineering, and Computer Science/Technology

Grade/Age Levels: Grades 6–12

Description: The Kopernik Observatory & Science Center offers weeklong camps for students in grades 6–12. Sponsored by the Link Foundation since 1994, in memory of local inventor/explorer Edwin A. Link, Link Summer STEM Exploration camps offer hands-on, high-tech adventures in science, technology, engineering, and math (STEM) that go beyond what is offered in school and give students the opportunity to explore a variety of STEM-related careers.

Kopernik camps bring together students with similar interests from across the region, giving them an opportunity to make friends from other school districts and have lots of fun, too! Camps have a maximum enrollment and many fill quickly each year. Visit the website for current offerings.

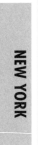

Pace Summer Scholars Institute

Contact: Ms. Dolores Alfieri, Program Coordinator

Address: Summer Scholars Program
Pace University
One Pace Plaza, Y-21
New York, NY 10038

Phone: 212-346-1697

Fax: 212-346-1948

E-mail: summerscholar@pace.edu

Website: http://www.pace.edu/summerscholars

Program Type: Academic Enrichment

Grade/Age Levels: Grades 10–11

Description: Pace University's Summer Scholars Institute is open to qualified high school rising sophomores and juniors who wish to experience college in New York City. They will live in dormitories, attend seminars taught by some of Pace University's best and brightest professors, participate in activities, and meet students who are equally interested in the NYC college experience. Each summer, we offer four different tracks in which students can major in during the week. Each track contains two sessions: one in the morning and one in the afternoon. Upon completion of the program, students will receive a certificate of course completion that will help strengthen college applications, in addition to the Pace Promise. Pace's promise is that all Summer Scholars will automatically receive a letter of recommendation from the Director of the Summer Scholars Institute for any college in which they apply, a $3,000 annual merit scholarship if they choose to attend Pace, and an automatic three elective course credits toward a Pace University degree.

Shoals Marine Laboratory Programs for High School Students

NEW YORK

Address: Shoals Marine Laboratory
Cornell University
106A Kennedy Hall
Ithaca, NY 14853

Phone: 603-862-5346

Fax: 603-862-0241

E-mail: shoals-lab@unh.edu

Website: http://www.sml.cornell.edu

Program Type: Math, Sciences, Engineering, and Computer Science/Technology

Grade/Age Levels: Grades 10–12

Description: Shoals Marine Laboratory offers the following summer courses for high school students. These are Cornell University courses and carry three Cornell University credits. Each course is 14 days long.

Marine Environmental Science for high school students focuses on coastal marine habitats, with an emphasis on issues as they relate to global habitats and concerns.

Advanced high school students/homeschooled students may be accepted to the undergraduate courses at Shoals. Please inquire.

The program is located at a marine residential field station located on Appledore Island in the Gulf of Maine. Students take an SML boat from Portsmouth, NH, to Appledore Island, ME. We offer immersion education in marine science and sustainability!

Summer at Rensselaer

Address: Summer at Rensselaer
Rensselaer Polytechnic Institute
110 8th St.
Troy, NY 12180

Phone: 518-276-6809

Fax: 518-276-8738

Website: http://summer.rpi.edu

Program Type: Academic Enrichment

Grade/Age Levels: Grades K–12

Description: Rensselaer Polytechnic Institute, a top technological university with an enthusiasm for innovation, offers an exciting summer experience for elementary, middle, or high school students. Summer credit courses are available to academically qualified high school students.

Summer in the City at Barnard

Contact: Ms. Ann Dachs, Director

Address: Pre-College Program
Barnard College
3009 Broadway
New York, NY 10027-6598

Phone: 212-854-8866

Fax: 212-854-8867

E-mail: pcp@barnard.edu

Website: http://www.barnard.edu/summer

Program Type: Academic Enrichment

Grade/Age Levels: Rising grades 11–12

Description: The Barnard College Summer in the City program offers young women a unique opportunity to get a taste of college life at one of the nation's premiere colleges, while exploring New York City both in and out of the classroom. Courses in 25+ subject areas ranging from entrepreneurship to dance, will allow you the opportunity to explore an area of interest on a deeper level through both in-class discussion and city exploration. Enjoy field trips and excursions to every corner of New York City, as well as Admissions and Career Development workshops on campus.

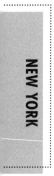

Summerfuel Programs in the U.S. and Abroad

Contact: Marissa Bates, Director

Address: Summerfuel Programs
19 West 21st St. Ste. 702
New York, NY 10010

Phone: 800-752-2250

Fax: 212-334-4934

E-mail: info@summerfuel.com

Website: http://www.summerfuel.com

Program Type: Foreign Language; Gap Year/Study Abroad/International Travel

Grade/Age Levels: Grades 9–12

Description: Summerfuel programs balance expert instruction and scheduled activities with excursions and freedom to foster greater independence and personal growth. Summerfuel offers the following programs:

» Pre-College Programs in Boston at Harvard University, in Amherst at the University of Massachusetts-Amherst, in Berkeley at University of California-Berkeley, and in Oxford at Oxford University for grades 9–12.
» Social Entrepreneurship Programs at Yale University and Stanford University for grades 9–12.
» College Admissions Prep at Columbia University, Tufts University, and University of California-Berkeley for grades 10–11.
» Language & Cultural Immersion Programs in Spain and France.

SUNY Oneonta Biological Field Station (BFS) Internships

NEW YORK

Contact: Dr. Willard Harman, Director

Address: High School Internships
Biological Field Station
5838 State Highway 80
Cooperstown, NY 13326

Phone: 607-547-8778

Fax: 607-547-5114

E-mail: willard.harman@oneonta.edu

Website: http://www.oneonta.edu/academics/biofld/internships.asp

Program Type: Math, Sciences, Engineering, and Computer Science/Technology

Grade/Age Levels: Ages 16 and up

Description: The Biological Field Station (BFS) at State University of New York (SUNY) at Oneonta offers high school internships. These sponsored internships last 9 weeks and run 5 days per week, 8 a.m. to 4 p.m. Interns are mentored and assigned a unique module of work as part of a team of researchers including faculty, staff, and undergraduate and graduate students focusing on specific areas of concern such as water quality monitoring, fisheries management, biological control studies, and surveys. All students participating are responsible for organizing and executing a project under the guidance of BFS faculty and staff. High school interns receive stipends of $1,750.

Telluride Association Summer Programs

Address: Telluride Association
217 West Ave.
Ithaca, NY 14850

Phone: 607-273-5011

Fax: 607-272-2667

E-mail: telluride@cornell.edu

Website: http://www.tellurideassociation.org

Program Type: Academic Enrichment

Grade/Age Levels: Grades 10–11

Description: The Telluride Association Sophomore Seminars (TASS) bring together intellectually motivated high school sophomores for 6-week-long summer programs on the campuses of Indiana University in Bloomington, IN; the University of Michigan in Ann Arbor, MI; and Cornell University in Ithaca, NY. By focusing on intense intellectual exploration within the field of African-American Studies and by selecting many of its students from urban populations underrepresented in similar learning environments, the TASS provides a challenging educational experience that is not easily available to high school students.

Telluride Association Summer Program for Juniors (TASP) is a 6-week educational experience for high school juniors that offers challenges and rewards rarely encountered in secondary school or even college. Each program is designed to bring together young people from around the world who share a passion for learning. TASP students, or TASPers, attend a seminar led by college and university faculty members and participate in many other educational and social activities outside the classroom.

Description, Continued

Every student awarded a place in a TASS or TASP attends the program on a full housing, dining, and tuition scholarship. Students pay only the costs of transportation and incidental expenses. Financial aid to cover transportation and lost summer earnings is available to students with demonstrated need.

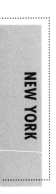

Union College Educating Girls for Engineering (EDGE) Workshop

Contact: Cherrice Traver, Professor of Electrical and Computer Engineering

Address: Department of Electrical
and Computer Engineering
Union College, 212 Steinmetz Hall
807 Union St.
Schenectady, NY 12308

Phone: 518-388-6326

E-mail: traverc@union.edu

Website: http://engineering.union.edu/edge

Program Type: Academic Enrichment; Math, Sciences, Engineering, and Computer Science/Technology

Grade/Age Levels: Rising grades 10–12

Description: The Union College EDGE program is an intensive, 2-week residential program for select rising high school sophomores, juniors, and seniors from across the country, taught by Union faculty and high school teachers. The program combines real-life college learning and living experiences with activities intended to interest girls in studying science and engineering in college and undertaking a career in one of those disciplines. More broadly, it is EDGE's intent to help redress the serious and continuing underrepresentation of women in engineering.

The program includes three mini courses and several off-campus educational trips that allow participants to see engineering design at work. Interested applicants must have completed yearlong high school math and science courses.

Union College Robot Camp

Contact: James Hedrick, Camp Director

Address: Union College Robot Camp
Department of Electrical
and Computer Engineering
Union College
Schenectady, NY 12308

Phone: 518-388-8027

E-mail: hedrickj@union.edu

Website: http://logopolis.union.edu/RobotCamp

Program Type: Academic Enrichment; Math, Sciences, Engineering, and Computer Science/Technology

Grade/Age Levels: Rising grades 7–12

Description: Robot Camp introduces middle school and high school students to the exciting world of robotics. Students learn to solder and program in Basic as they take a box of parts and transform them into a working robot. The weeklong camp also includes sessions on robotics in general and demonstrations of robots developed at Union College. The camp culminates in an exhibition for parents and the public at the Schenectady Museum, where students showcase their work.

University of Rochester Pre-College Programs

Contact: Ursula Balent, Pre-College Programs Manager

Address: University of Rochester
Office of Pre-College Programs
Box 270034
Rochester, NY 14627-0034

Phone: 585-275-3221

Fax: 585-756-8480

E-mail: precollege@rochester.edu

Website: http://enrollment.rochester.edu/precollege

Program Type: Academic Enrichment

Grade/Age Levels: Rising Grades 9–12

Description: The University of Rochester's innovative precollege programs have been enlightening young minds for more than 20 years. High school students are able to gain new perspectives on their academic abilities and potential, get a taste of the college environment, enjoy new opportunities to investigate educational goals, and build lasting relationships with peers who share similar academic and personal interests. All courses are designed to broaden the educational experience and sharpen academic skills, helping students learn more about who—not just what—they want to be. Visit the website for current offerings.

All-Arts, Sciences and Technology Camp

Address: All-Arts, Sciences and Technology Camp
Division of Continual Learning
UNCG
P.O. Box 26170
Greensboro, NC 27402-6170

Phone: 336-315-7044; 866-334-2255

Fax: 336-315-7737

E-mail: allarts@uncg.edu

Website: http://allarts.uncg.edu

Program Type: Academic Enrichment

Grade/Age Levels: Ages 7–15

Description: The All-Arts, Sciences and Technology Camp is a weeklong summer camp designed to give in-depth, hands-on instruction in the arts, sciences, and technology. The camp also includes recreation, citizenship, and multicultural entertainment. Each camper attends a morning class and an afternoon class chosen from a wide variety of course offerings that suit individual tastes and preferences. The class size is small, and the curriculum encourages problem solving and critical thinking.

Duke University Talent Identification Program (TIP) Summer Programs

Address: Duke University TIP
1121 W. Main St.
Durham, NC 27701-2028

Phone: 919-668-9100

E-mail: information@tip.duke.edu

Website: http://www.tip.duke.edu

Program Type: Academic Enrichment; Leadership/Service/Volunteer; Gap Year/Study Abroad/International Travel

Grade/Age Levels: Grades 5–12

Description: The Duke University Talent Identification Program (Duke TIP) is a nonprofit organization dedicated to serving academically gifted and talented youth. As a world leader in gifted and talented education, Duke TIP works with students, their families, and educators to identify, recognize, challenge, engage, and help students reach their highest potential. Duke TIP offers several challenging summer educational adventures to motivated, dedicated, and talented students who possess a desire to learn.

CRISIS is a summer residential program for current fifth and sixth graders. Through problem-based learning, CRISIS will build leadership and teamwork skills by asking students to assume the role of a professional on a research team, collaborating with team members to solve a community crisis. They will explore a field such as engineering, business, medicine, or health, while participating in leadership and development activities designed to help participants discover more about who they are and what they want to be.

Description, Continued

Summer Studies Programs are superb academic opportunities and dynamic residential and social experiences for 7th through 10th graders. These 3-week sessions are intense and demanding; students are challenged to think critically about themselves and their world.

Field Studies are 2 weeks long and take place in U.S. locales or in countries around the world such as China, Costa Rica, and the Netherlands. These authentic academic experiences, similar to college field courses, allow students to take advantage of unique surroundings to fully explore the course material.

eStudies connects gifted students with peers and with a Duke TIP instructor as they pursue challenging academic coursework delivered over the Internet via Sakai, a world-class learning management system. Classes are offered in summer.

For more information about eligibility requirements, costs, deadlines, and applications, please visit the website.

Duke University Youth Programs

Address: Duke University Youth Programs
Duke Continuing Studies
Bishop's House Room 205
Box 90700
Durham, NC 27708-0700

Phone: 919-684-2827

Fax: 919-681-8235

E-mail: youth@duke.edu

Website: http://www.learnmore.duke.edu/youth

Program Type: Academic Enrichment

Grade/Age Levels: Rising grades 5 and up

Description: Several programs, dates vary. Programs have included Action Science Camp for Young Women, Biosciences and Engineering Camp, Computer Camp, W.R.I.T.E. for College, Math Camp, IMAGINE . . . Leading by Example!, Young Writers' Camp, Creative Writers' Workshop, and Constructing Your College Experience. All programs seek to engage learners in innovative, interactive, transformative learning experiences. Co-curricular social and recreational activities are carefully planned and delivered to complement the instructional day. The program offers a limited number of need-based partial scholarships.

Green River Preserve Summer Camp and Expeditions

Contact: Anne and Stephen Mead

Address: 301 Green River Rd.
Cedar Mountain, NC 28718

Phone: 828-698-8828

Fax: 828-698-9201

E-mail: info@greenriverpreserve.org

Website: http://www.greenriverpreserve.org

Program Type: Academic Enrichment; Leadership/Service/Volunteer

Grade/Age Levels: Rising grade 9–college freshmen

Description: Green River Preserve Expeditions are teen adventure camps offering transformational life experiences and leadership training. Based on a foundation of respect, groups of up to 12 participants in rising 9th grade to college freshmen and their leaders embark on 2–3-week adventure trips in one of our four expedition sites: Blue Ridge, a 2-week backpacking and whitewater canoe trip in the Blue Ridge Mountains of Western North Carolina: Outer Banks, a 2-week backpacking and sea kayaking trip on the Outer Banks of North Carolina; Trail Blazers, a 3-week leadership service trip including a backpacking and canoe trip; and Western Expeditions, a 3-week backpacking and white water rafting trip in the San Juan Mountains of Southwest Colorado.

Green River Preserve and Queens University of Charlotte, NC, have partnered together to offer four college credit hours for Western Expeditions (WXP) and Trailblazers Leadership Expedition (TBX). These Expeditions are for rising 11th and 12th graders and college freshmen.

Description, Continued

Green River Preserve Expedition Camps offer quality, intentional, experiential learning opportunities that spark diversity of thought and creativity. Campers discover themselves, face their fears, and gain GRIT. They build life skills such as self-confidence, social achievement, teamwork, and leadership. They become their Best Me!

July Experience at Davidson College

Contact: Ms. Evelyn Gerdes, Director

Address: Davidson July Experience
Davidson College
P.O. Box 7151
Davidson, NC 28035

Phone: 704-894-2508

Fax: 704-894-2059

E-mail: julyexp@davidson.edu

Website: http://www.davidson.edu/julyexperience

Program Type: Academic Enrichment

Grade/Age Levels: Grades 11–12

Description: July Experience at Davidson College is a powerful summer academic experience for rising high school juniors and seniors. Participants spend 3 weeks at Davidson College, located just north of Charlotte, NC, being challenged by courses taught by Davidson faculty, living in residence halls with students from across the country and around the world, while participating in Davidson College traditions led by counselors/mentors who are current Davidson students. July Experience need-based scholarships are available.

North Carolina State University Engineering Summer Programs

Address: Engineering Summer Programs
North Carolina State University
College of Engineering
Campus Box 7904, 120 Page Hall
Raleigh, NC 27695-7904

Phone: 919-515-3263

Fax: 919-515-8702

Website: http://www.engr.ncsu.edu/theengineeringplace/summerprograms

Program Type: Math, Sciences, Engineering, and Computer Science/Technology

Grade/Age Levels: Day Camps: Rising grades 3–10; Residential Camps: Rising grades 11 and 12

Description: North Carolina State University offers residential camps for rising 11th and 12th graders and day camps for rising 3rd through 10th graders. In the residential camps, students spend a week on campus, live in the dorms, eat in the dining halls, meet like-minded students from all over the globe, and immerse themselves in a specific engineering workshop of their choosing. In the day camps, students are introduced to a variety of engineering fields through fun, yet challenging, hands-on projects and investigations. By the end of the week, they have a deeper understanding of the field of engineering and related career opportunities. We also offer day camps in various partnering camp locations in North Carolina.

University of North Carolina School of the Arts Summer Session

Address: UNCSA Educational Outreach
and Summer Programs
1533 South Main St.
Winston-Salem, NC 27127

Phone: 336-734-2848

E-mail: summer@uncsa.edu

Website: http://www.uncsa.edu/summer

Program Type: Fine, Performing, and Visual Arts

Grade/Age Levels: Grades 7 and up

Description: Welcome to the University of North Carolina School of the Arts, where summer is intense, exhilarating, and all about the students. Whether your passion is dance, drama, filmmaking, music, or visual arts, you'll find all the hands-on experience, all the performance opportunities, and all the individual attention from professional artists you've dared to dream of.

Auditions are required for dance and music intensives. The program offers both residential and commuter options.

UNCW MarineQuest

Contact:	Dr. Sue Kezios, Director
Address:	University of North Carolina Wilmington 601 South College Rd. Wilmington, NC 28403
Phone:	910-962-2640
Fax:	910-962-2410
E-mail:	marinequest@uncw.edu
Website:	http://www.uncw.edu/marinequest
Program Type:	Math, Sciences, Engineering, and Computer Science/Technology; Fine, Performing, and Visual Arts; Internships/Paid Positions; Leadership/Service/Volunteer
Grade/Age Levels:	Ages 4–17
Description:	MarineQuest's mission is to offer programming that provides young people with opportunities to explore, discover, and value our marine habitats and encourages them to develop into environmentally responsible adults. To achieve this, we offer more than 25 different summer academic enrichment programs for ages 4–17. Each camp explores the four fields of marine science and exposes campers to current events and environmental issues in marine science. Depending on the camp, we provide experiences with kayaking, diving, marine engineering, and scientific research, including research cruises. We offer specialty programs in environmental art and documentary videography, marine technology of ROVs, marine biotechnology, service learning, and leadership. We also offer single-gender camp options for all ages. All of our lessons and activities are designed to make the learning process fun and engaging and are based on the research of University of North Carolina Wilmington scientists.

North Dakota Governor's Schools

Contact: Mr. Ryan Niemann,
Academic Events Coordinator

Address: North Dakota Governor's Schools
North Dakota State University
314 Family Life Center
Fargo, ND 58108-6050

Phone: 701-231-6727

E-mail: Ryan.Niemann@ndsu.edu

Website: http://www.ndsu.edu/govschool

Program Type: Math, Sciences, Engineering, and Computer Science/Technology; Fine, Performing, and Visual Arts

Grade/Age Levels: Rising grades 11–12

Description: North Dakota Governor's Schools is a 6-week residential program for scholastically motivated North Dakota high school sophomores and juniors. Students live, work, and have fun on NDSU's campus. Governor's Schools academic programs offer high-quality, concentrated instruction from NDSU faculty through classroom experiences, discussion groups, labs, field trips, and other activities.

ASM Materials Camp

Contact: Ms. Jeane Deatherage,
Administrator of Foundation Programs

Address: ASM Materials Education Foundation
9639 Kinsman Rd.
Materials Park, OH 44073-0002

Phone: 440-338-5151 ext. 5533

Fax: 440-338-4634

E-mail: jeane.deatherage@asminternational.org

Website: http://www.asminternational.org/about/foundation/students/materials-camps

Program Type: Math, Sciences, Engineering, and Computer Science/Technology

Grade/Age Levels: Grades 11–12

Description: This weeklong academic camp features highly interactive, lab-based activity tailored to the individual interest areas of students entering their junior or senior year in high school. Highly motivated inquisitive learners with math and science aptitude should apply. The strongest applicants will have a basic knowledge of algebra, chemistry, and physics and will show a strong interest in applied science and demonstrate a desire to pursue a college major and career in engineering and/or materials science. This camp is free to participants.

Kenyon Review Young Writers Summer Program

Contact: Ms. Anna Duke Reach, Director of Programs

Address: Kenyon Review Young Writers
Finn House
102 W. Wiggin St.
Kenyon College
Gambier, OH 43022

Phone: 740-427-5207

Fax: 740-427-5417

E-mail: youngwriters@kenyonreview.org

Website: http://www.kenyonreview.org/workshops/young-writers

Program Type: Academic Enrichment

Grade/Age Levels: Ages 16–18

Description: The Kenyon Review Young Writers Program is an intensive, 2-week workshop for intellectually curious, motivated high school students who value writing. Young Writers takes place at Kenyon College, a leading liberal arts college renowned for its tradition of literary study. The goal of the program is to help students develop their creative and critical abilities with language in order to become more productive writers and more insightful thinkers. Workshop groups (each with no more than 13 students) led by experienced writing instructors meet for 5 hours a day. In addition to free writing exercises and responses to prompts, students write stories, poetry, personal narratives, dialogues, reflective passages, and experimental pieces. Participants live in Kenyon College residential halls and have full access to computer labs and recreational facilities. Evening and weekend activities include readings by prominent writers.

Miami University Summer Scholars Program

Contact:	Lindsey Holden, Summer Scholars Program Coordinator
Address:	Summer Scholars Program Miami University Office of Admission 301 S. Campus Ave. Oxford, OH 45056
Phone:	513-529-2559
Fax:	513-529-1550
E-mail:	summerscholars@miamioh.edu
Website:	http://miamioh.edu/summerscholars
Program Type:	Academic Enrichment
Grade/Age Levels:	Rising grades 11 and 12

Description: The Summer Scholars Program provides a rich, early college experience for academically talented rising high school juniors and seniors from across the globe. Students will join an engaged community of learners for an intense, 2-week program in which they do the following:

» Participate in challenging, immersive academic modules centered on a specific topic or area of interest.

» Learn alongside our leading faculty and professional experts.

» Reside in a "living-learning" community with other Summer Scholars participants and get a real preview of college life—live in a residence hall, eat in our award-winning dining halls, and enjoy campus facilities such as our Recreational Sports Center and Goggin Ice Center.

» Attend special workshops on topics such as the college admission process and financial assistance. Get an insider's look

OHIO

Description, Continued

at the college application process—learn about ACT/SAT test preparation, how to find the right college fit, how to write the best college essay, as well as get an introduction to financial aid and scholarships.

- Participate in special excursions to local attractions, such as Kings Island and a local baseball game.
- Receive priority consideration for merit scholarships and for selection to top programs such as the University Academic Scholars Program and the University Honors Program.

Ross Mathematics Program

Contact: Daniel Shapiro, Director

Address: Ross Mathematics Program
OSU Department of Mathematics
231 W. 18th Ave.
Columbus, OH 43210

Phone: 614-292-5101

Fax: 614-292-1479

E-mail: ross@math.osu.edu

Website: http://www.math.osu.edu/ross

Program Type: Math, Sciences, Engineering, and Computer Science/Technology

Grade/Age Levels: Ages 15–18

Description: The Ross Program at the Ohio State University is an intensive summer experience designed to encourage motivated precollege students to explore mathematics. During this 6-week residential program, students are immersed in a world of mathematical discovery. This program is sponsored by the university in partnership with the Clay Mathematics Institute.

Wright State University Summer Enrichment Programs

Contact: Ms. Elizabeth Turner, Assistant Director

Address: Wright State University
Office of Pre-College Programs
3640 Colonel Glenn Hwy.
Dayton, OH 45435-0001

Phone: 937-775-3135

Fax: 937-775-4883

E-mail: precollege@wright.edu

Website: http://wright.edu/precollege

Program Type: Academic Enrichment

Grade/Age Levels: Grades 6–12

Description: The Office of Pre-College Programs offers students entering grades 6–12 the opportunity to attend summer residential enrichment programs. Courses are offered on the following topics: aviation, creative writing, leadership, mathematics, science, television production, theatre, and many more. Each program is comprised of a variety of learning experiences including lectures, hands-on projects, field trips, small-group discussions, and learning community activities. Dormitory life, recreation, and social events promote friendships and social interaction among participants. Programs are taught by university faculty, staff, or experts from the local community. Each program has limited enrollment, so register early.

Oklahoma City University (OCU) Summer Music Programs

Contact: Ms. JoBeth Moad, Director

Address: OCU Summer Music Programs
Performing Arts Academy
Oklahoma City University
2501 N. Blackwelder
Oklahoma City, OK 73106

Phone: 405-208-5410

Fax: 405-208-5218

E-mail: academy@okcu.edu; jmoad@okcu.edu

Website: http://www.okcu.edu/music/performing-arts-academy/summer

Program Type: Fine, Performing, and Visual Arts

Grade/Age Levels: Grades 7–12

Description: Each summer, students travel from across the United States and around the world to the Oklahoma City University campus to participate in the Performing Arts Academy's Summer Music Programs. These intensive precollege programs are designed for serious students who want to develop their talents and be challenged by OCU's high standards. The programs are chiefly directed and instructed by faculty from OCU's outstanding Bass School of Music and TheatreOCU. Participants receive the training that has produced Tony, Grammy and Emmy award winners such as two-time Tony nominee and Tony-award winner Kristin Chenoweth, three-time Tony nominee Kelli O'Hara, Emmy nominated Ron Raines, Metropolitan Opera legend Leona Mitchell, award-winning guitarist Edgar Cruz, and Grammy and Emmy winner Mason Williams.

Oregon Museum of Science & Industry Camps

Address: Oregon Museum of Science & Industry
1945 SE Water Ave.
Portland, OR 97214

Phone: 503-797-4000

Fax: 503-239-7800

E-mail: register@omsi.edu

Website: http://www.omsi.edu

Program Type: Math, Sciences, Engineering, and Computer Science/Technology

Grade/Age Levels: Ages 7–18

Description: OMSI Camps are overnight, residential programs that take place in beautiful settings ranging from the mountains to the coast to the desert, and offer the perfect combination of science, adventure, and fun. Campers may sleep under the towering redwoods in California, raft a river in central Oregon, backpack through an alpine forest, or search for whales on San Juan Island. Camps are for students entering grades 2–12.

OMSI Classes are weeklong day programs that challenge kids to investigate, invent, experiment, interpret, theorize, discover, and share what they learn with others. Topics include chemistry, biology, astronomy, computer science, animation, engineering, geology, rocketry, and more. Classes are for students entering grades K–8.

OMSI Family camps are weekend programs that offer adventure for all ages. Program offerings offer opportunities for the whole family to explore together in a variety of settings such as the coast or the John Day Fossil Beds. See the website for exact dates and locations.

Saturday Academy Apprenticeships in Science and Engineering (ASE)

Address: Saturday Academy
5000 N Willamette Blvd.
Portland, OR 97203

Phone: 503-200-5861; 503-200-5858

Fax: 503-200-5899

E-mail: ase@saturdayacademy.org

Website: http://www.saturdayacademy.org/ase

Program Type: Math, Sciences, Engineering, and Computer Science/Technology

Grade/Age Levels: Grades 9–11

Description: Apprenticeships in Science and Engineering (ASE) is part of Saturday Academy, a nonprofit organization based in Portland, OR. Students participate in ASE for 8-week, full-time, summer internships at various locations throughout the state under the guidance of mentors in different fields of science and engineering. Students apply in late winter. Start and end dates are flexible but must occur during the summer school break. Participation in two conferences is mandatory. Housing is the responsibility of apprentices and parents, should the apprentice be selected for a position beyond commuting distance.

University of Oregon Summer Enrichment Program

Address: Summer Enrichment Program
University of Oregon
1859 E. 15th Ave.
Eugene, OR 97403

Phone: 541-346-3084

Fax: 541-346-3594

E-mail: sep@uoregon.edu

Website: http://uoyetag.uoregon.edu/summer-programs/sep-html

Program Type: Academic Enrichment

Grade/Age Levels: Grades 6–10

Description: The University of Oregon's Summer Enrichment Program (SEP) attracts thousands of academically motivated middle and high school kids from around the world seeking educational challenge. Students participate in exceptional learning experiences and engage in meaningful social and recreational opportunities in a university environment. SEP is a remarkable place where students meet others with similar interests and talents, share their love of learning with others who value creativity and intelligence, and have lots of fun making new friends and memories that last a lifetime—all while experiencing firsthand what it's like to become a student at the University of Oregon.

Students live on campus in small groups of 12–14 others of the same gender and age. Each group is assigned a Residential Adult and Junior Counselor. The student-to-staff ratio of 10 to 1 allows SEP to address specific needs of each age group and every individual. Students spend time after classes relaxing

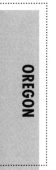

Description, Continued

with friends, shopping in local campus stores, and participating in recreational indoor and outdoor activities. Evenings and weekends provide even more choices including: creative problem solving competitions, game night, visiting the local Saturday market, a costume dance, and more! Special events such as talent shows and comedy skits make for an amazing, memorable experience.

Students attend six classes located throughout the campus during the 2-week program. The classes offered cover a variety of subjects, including advanced mathematics, science, law, visual arts, dance, theater, music, literature, engineering, history, technology, languages, cultural studies, and creative writing (course topics vary annually). Curriculum is advanced early high school to advanced early college level in difficulty. Courses are challenging, hands-on, nontraditional, and are not available in public schools. There are no exams or homework. Students are encouraged to develop interest in the material and create dialogue with peers in order to drive their learning.

Allegheny College Summer Programs

Contact: Rebecca Wiler Ward, Director

Address: Allegheny College Summer Programs
520 N. Main St.
Box V
Meadville, PA 16335

Phone: 814-332-3101

Fax: 814-332-2837

E-mail: rward@allegheny.edu

Website: http://sites.allegheny.edu/conference/summer-programs

Program Type: Academic Enrichment

Grade/Age Levels: Ages 3–18

Description: Allegheny College offers various educational opportunities during the summer months for elementary and high school students. The summer of 2014, for example, included Creating Landscapes for teens, Creek Camp for high school students, and a variety of sports camps for children and high school students on topics such as music, dance, and athletics.

Daniel Fox Summer Scholars Camps

Contact: Ms. Susan Greenawall, Summer Camps Administrative Assistant

Address: Daniel Fox Summer Scholars Camps
Lebanon Valley College
101 N. College Ave.
Annville, PA 17003

Phone: 717-867-6193; 877-877-0423

Fax: 717-867-6018

E-mail: greenawa@lvc.edu

Website: http://www.lvc.edu/youth-scholars

Program Type: Academic Enrichment

Grade/Age Levels: Rising grades 10 and up

Description: The Summer Scholars program is a residential experience for exceptional high school students who have completed 9th, 10th, or 11th grade, with participants completing challenging academic activities, learning about career opportunities in their chosen fields, gaining knowledge as to how to successfully navigate the social side of college life, and demonstrating to others a firm interest in higher education.

Students spend a week experiencing life at a college known for its atmosphere of academic excellence and personal attention—a college chosen by *U.S. News & World Report* as one of the top ranked schools in the North in the "Great Schools, Great Prices" category, and by *The Princeton Review* as one of the "Best Northeastern Colleges."

Beyond preparing students for collegiate life, a Summer Scholars Camp develops students' long-term interests in their selected disciplines. Past participants have entered careers involving school counseling, clinical psychology, veterinary medicine, and pharmaceutical research, as well as many others, and participants have expressed the impact of the program on their lives.

Penn State Abington Kids & Teen College

Contact: Deanna Bosley, Director

Address: Pennsylvania State University,
Abington College
Cloverly Building
1600 Woodland Rd.
Abington, PA 19001-3990

Phone: 215-881-7400

Fax: 215-881-7412

E-mail: dlb61@psu.edu

Website: http://www.abington.psu.edu/youthteen

Program Type: Academic Enrichment

Grade/Age Levels: Grades 3–12

Description: Penn State Abington's Kids & Teen College offers fun, enriching, and educational week-long programs for students entering grades 3–12. The campus offers a wide range of programs that focus on many academic subject areas. Topics range from science, robotics, engineering, and computer camps to literature, theater, public speaking, and art. Many of the summer camps provide students opportunities to learn about various professions and careers, including engineering, veterinary medicine, health care, multimedia design, astrobiology, and meteorology.

LEADership, Education, and Development (LEAD) Summer Programs

Address: LEAD Programs & Alumni Relations
500 Office Center Dr., Ste. 400
Fort Washington, PA 19034

Phone: 215-261-7001

Website: http://www.leadprogram.org

Program Type: Academic Enrichment

Grade/Age Levels: Grades 8–11

Description: Students can explore their interest in the fields of business, engineering, or computer science through a fun and challenging LEAD Summer Institute. Acceptance into one of the highly-competitive, 2–4-week Summer Institutes puts students on the path to:

» receive hands-on experience in business or engineering at one of the nation's leading universities,
» hear firsthand from executives at the top companies in the world,
» reside and attend classes on campus and attend unique cultural events,
» build relationships with peers from around the country who share your interests and aspirations,
» connect with LEAD alumni who can serve as mentors in college and professional life, and
» learn about internships, employment opportunities, and special events available to LEAD alumni.

Visit the website for dates and locations.

The Management & Technology Summer Institute (M&TSI)

Address: The Jerome Fisher Program in
Management & Technology
The Management & Technology
Summer Institute (M&TSI)
3537 Locust Walk, Ste. 100
Philadelphia, PA 19104

Phone: 215-898-4145

Fax: 215-573-7717

E-mail: mgtech@seas.upenn.edu

Website: http://www.upenn.edu/fisher/summer-mt

Program Type: Math, Sciences, Engineering, and Computer Science/Technology

Grade/Age Levels: Rising grade 12

Description: M&TSI is a 3-week for-credit summer program for rising high school seniors who want to learn about the integration of technological concepts and management principles. Sponsored by The Jerome Fisher Program in Management and Technology, the School of Engineering and Applied Science, and The Wharton School of the University of Pennsylvania, M&TSI features classes taught by leading faculty and successful entrepreneurs, field trips to companies and research and development facilities, and intensive team projects, as well as other activities designed to give students the opportunity to learn about the principles and practice of technological innovation.

Summer Study at Penn State University

Address: Summer Study Programs
900 Walt Whitman Rd.
Melville, NY 11747

Phone: 631-424-1000

Fax: 631-424-0567

E-mail: info@summerstudy.com

Website: http://www.summerstudy.com

Program Type: Academic Enrichment; Math, Sciences, Engineering, and Computer Science/Technology; Leadership/Service/Volunteer

Grade/Age Levels: Rising grades 10 and up

Description: A precollege program at any university is a wonderful summer experience and the Penn State summer study programs offered by Summer Study ensure the most exciting and educationally rewarding summer of your life! From 2-, 3 1/2-, and 5-week noncredit enrichment programs to a 6 1/2 week college credit precollege academic program, Penn State Summer Study programs offer an incredible summer filled with:

- challenging, yet fun classes,
- new friendships and personal growth,
- the finest Penn State sports and recreational facilities only available on a "Big Ten" campus,
- exciting nightlife in the "Ultimate College Town,"
- the adventure of weekend travel and the excitement of the Pennsylvania Arts Festival,
- an experienced precollege academic program staff who truly care about the needs of each individual student, and

Description, Continued

» thousands of college students on a campus that is very much "alive" and full of spirit.

PENNSYLVANIA

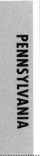

The University of the Arts Pre-College Summer Institute

Address: Pre-College Summer Institute
The University of the Arts
320 S. Broad St.
Philadelphia, PA 19102

Phone: 215-717-6430

Fax: 215-717-6538

E-mail: precollege@uarts.edu

Website: http://www.uarts.edu/summerinstitute

Program Type: Fine, Performing, and Visual Arts

Grade/Age Levels: Grades 9–12

Description: The 350 students who attend the Pre-College Summer Institute travel to Philadelphia from more than 25 states and numerous nations. They are creative, curious, talented, energetic, and excited about the arts. Our programs foster investigation and exploration of the principles of creativity and focus on the development of each individual student. The Pre-College Summer Institute will challenge your imagination and expose you to dynamic and interesting people, including your peers and instructors. This is both a residential and commuter program, varying from 1–4 weeks depending on program area.

Writers Workshop at Susquehanna University

Contact: Dr. Gary Fincke, Director

Address: Writers Workshop
Susquehanna University
610 University Ave.
Selinsgrove, PA 17870

Phone: 570-372-4164

Fax: 570-372-2741

E-mail: gfincke@susqu.edu

Website: http://www.susqu.edu/about/writers workshop.asp

Program Type: Academic Enrichment

Grade/Age Levels: Grades 11–12

Description: The Writers Workshop is open to experienced writers entering 11th or 12th grade. Writers Workshop attendees are chosen based on teacher/counselor recommendations and portfolio submissions, and each applicant is required to submit 5–6 poems or 6–8 pages of fiction/creative nonfiction.

The weeklong experience, now in its 25th summer, provides America's most talented high school writers with the opportunity to work in intensive, small-group workshops headed by nationally recognized authors. The Writers' Workshop features workshops in fiction, creative nonfiction, and poetry.

Summer Academy in Architecture

Contact: Sue Contente

Address: Summer Academy in Architecture
Roger Williams University
School of Architecture, Art,
and Historic Preservation
One Old Ferry Rd.
Bristol, RI 02809

Phone: 401-254-3683

E-mail: saahp@rwu.edu

Website: http://www.rwu.edu/academics/schools-colleges/saahp/special-programs/summer-programs/summer-academy

Program Type: Academic Enrichment

Grade/Age Levels: Grade 12

Description: The School of Architecture, Art, and Historic Preservation at Roger Williams University offers an intensive 4-week Summer Academy in Architecture for high school students who have successfully completed their sophomore or junior year of study. The program offers a curriculum with a variety of studio, seminar, and field experiences, extracurricular activities, and field trips, allowing students to understand architecture as a possible area of college study and as a career. Students gain a broader view of the field while developing skills and portfolio materials to add to their applications to professional school. Workshops, lectures, demonstrations, and off-campus experiences complement daily design studios. Students earn three college credits.

Carolina Journalism Institute

Address: Carolina Journalism Institute
University of South Carolina
School of Journalism and
Mass Communications
Columbia, SC 29208

Phone: 803-777-6284

Fax: 803-777-4103

E-mail: schopres@mailbox.sc.edu

Website: http://www.sc.edu/cmcis/so/cji/index.html

Program Type: Academic Enrichment

Grade/Age Levels: Grades 6–12

Description: This intensive 5-day regional workshop helps middle and high school students and advisers sharpen their skills in publication, production, interviewing, writing, editing, design, and leadership for broadcast, literary magazines, newspapers, and yearbooks. Participants will attend large-group sessions and individual classes that focus on broadcast, business, desktop publishing, journalistic writing, literary magazine, newspaper, photojournalism, and yearbook. Both beginning and advanced classes are offered.

Summer Scholars Program at Furman University

Address: Summer Scholars Program
Furman University
3300 Poinsett Highway
Greenville, SC 29613

Phone: 864-294-3231

Fax: 864-294-2018

E-mail: summer.scholars@furman.edu

Website: http://www.furman.edu/admission

Program Type: Academic Enrichment

Grade/Age Levels: Grades 11–12

Description: Furman University's Summer Scholars Programs are one-week academic enrichment programs designed for rising juniors and seniors in high school. Students study under the direction of Furman faculty members in small-group settings. Summer Scholars programs typically include a variety of learning experiences such as lectures, class discussions, debates, laboratory experiences, field trips, group and individual projects, and other activities intended to provide an enjoyable and challenging learning experience for participants.

University of South Carolina Summer Dance Conservatory

Contact: Kerri Lambert, Administrative Director

Address: SC Summer Dance Conservatory
University of South Carolina
324 Sumter St.
Columbia, SC 29208

Phone: 803-777-7264

Fax: 803-777-0837

E-mail: klambert@mailbox.sc.edu

Website: http://artsandsciences.sc.edu/dance/sc-summer-dance-conservatory

Program Type: Fine, Performing, and Visual Arts

Grade/Age Levels: Ages 11 and up

Description: The South Carolina Summer Dance Conservatory is a 3-week residential or commuter youth program offering intensive training in classical ballet or contemporary dance/jazz. Acceptance is by audition for ages 11 years and older. DVD auditions are permitted. Visit our website for audition sites and times.

South Dakota Ambassadors of Excellence Program

Contact:	Andrea Wange, Director
Address:	South Dakota Ambassadors of Excellence Program The University of South Dakota Division of Curriculum and Instruction School of Education 414 E. Clark St. Vermillion, SD 57069
Phone:	605-677-5828
Fax:	605-677-3102
E-mail:	gifted@usd.edu
Website:	http://www.usd.edu/education/gifted-camp/ambassadors-of-excellence-program.cfm
Program Type:	Leadership/Service/Volunteer
Grade/Age Levels:	Grades 10–12
Description:	This summer program is designed for selected former South Dakota Governor's Camp participants and other students of high ability in rising grades 10–12. The mission is to provide an optimum learning experience for South Dakota's gifted high school students in a safe and supportive environment, emphasizing service, leadership, and artistic potential. The program includes team-building activities, educational exploratory sessions, a community service project, and more.

South Dakota Governor's Camp

Contact: Andrea Wange, Director

Address: South Dakota Governor's Camp
The University of South Dakota
Division of Curriculum and Instruction
School of Education
414 E. Clark St.
Vermillion, SD 57069

Phone: 605-677-5828

Fax: 605-677-3102

E-mail: trudi.nelson@usd.edu

Website: http://www.usd.edu/education/gifted-camp/sd-governors-camp.cfm

Program Type: Academic Enrichment

Grade/Age Levels: Grades 7–9

Description: The mission of the South Dakota Governor's Camp is to provide an optimum learning experience for bright children in a safe and supportive environment. The Governor's Camp provides academic enrichment experiences with USD faculty and trained staff. Students participate in recreational programs using campus facilities and have a full schedule of challenging activities with other bright students.

Research Experience for High School Students (REHSS)

Contact: Dr. Kimberly Mulligan, Program Coordinator

Address: Vanderbilt Center for Science Outreach
PMB 407831
1400 18th Avenue South, First Floor
Nashville, TN 37240-7831

Phone: 615-332-7140

Fax: 615-322-7169

E-mail: kimberly.x.mulligan@vanderbilt.edu

Website: http://www.vanderbilt.edu/cso/rehss/

Program Type: Math, Sciences, Engineering, and Computer Science/Technology

Grade/Age Levels: Rising grade 12; must be at least 16 years old

Description: The Research Experience for High School Students (formerly Research Internship Program) is an intense, 6-week scientific research internship at Vanderbilt University, centering on full immersion in a Vanderbilt University or Vanderbilt University Medical Center research lab. Students engage in an independent research project under the mentorship of a research faculty member at Vanderbilt.

All REHSS participants also attend weekly breakout sessions as a group, led by a team of Vanderbilt faculty, postdoctoral researchers, and graduate students. These breakout sessions complement the student's lab experience by developing skill sets for scientific communication and comprehension, as well as expose students to the Vanderbilt research community, scientific careers, and university studies.

Description, Continued

REHSS culminates with an end-of-summer research symposium where students will present their projects in a public research poster forum, consistent with national scientific meetings.

Students are accepted through a competitive application process that includes a phone interview. The summer research experience is intense but highly rewarding. If you enjoy science and have a strong desire to explore and discover the world around you, we are looking for you. It may be the best summer you've ever had!

Summer Academy at Vanderbilt for the Young (SAVY)

Address: PMB 0506
230 Appleton Pl.
Nashville, TN 37203-5721

Phone: 615-322-8261

Fax: 615-322-3457

E-mail: savy.pty@vanderbilt.edu

Website: http://pty.vanderbilt.edu

Program Type: Math, Sciences, Engineering, and Computer Science/Technology

Grade/Age Levels: Rising grades 1–7

Description: The Summer Academy at Vanderbilt for the Young (SAVY) is a day program that provides a dynamic, fast-paced curriculum experience to qualifying gifted children in rising first–seventh grades. SAVY courses are accelerated and are designed for academically gifted students who test at the 95th percentile and above on a standardized achievement or ability test. Vanderbilt professors, master teachers, and graduate students offer accelerated SAVY courses that cover a wide variety of high interest topics, including humanities, science, math, and writing courses. SAVY includes small, hands-on classes designed for the exceptionally talented and motivated learner. Class size is limited to approximately 12 students for grades 1–3 classes and approximately 15 students for grades 4–7. Some of our summer course offerings include creative writing, genetics, cultural anthropology, social psychology, algebra, and neuroscience. SAVY is a place where high-ability students are able to work together alongside content experts. Need-based financial aid is available.

Vanderbilt Summer Academy (VSA)

Contact: Laura McLean, Admissions Coordinator, Vanderbilt Programs for Talented Youth

Address: PMB 506
230 Appleton Pl.
Nashville, TN 37203-5721

Phone: 615-322-8261

Fax: 615-322-3457

E-mail: vsa.pty@vanderbilt.edu

Website: http://pty.vanderbilt.edu/students/vsa

Program Type: Math, Sciences, Engineering, and Computer Science/Technology

Grade/Age Levels: Rising grades 8–12

Description: At Vanderbilt Summer Academy (VSA), highly gifted students learn at an accelerated pace in a community of their like-ability peers. Students live on the Vanderbilt freshman campus and enroll in advanced courses with Vanderbilt professors and scholars. Courses promote academic discourse, habits of content experts, and advanced process skills within specific disciplines. These hands-on courses may consist of going on rounds with doctors at Vanderbilt University Medical Center, studying nanotechnology with a Ph.D. candidate in an engineering lab, culling through Vanderbilt's Civil War archives, or speaking with a published author who will help students get started on the next bestselling novel. Outside the classroom, VSA's residential staff provides unique social and recreational activities, including special seminars on the college admissions process and college life, as well as field trips around Nashville, to make sure students have an amazing Vanderbilt learning experience. Need-based financial aid is available.

Vanderbilt University PAVE

Contact: Dr. John Veillette, Associate Dean and Director of PAVE

Address: Vanderbilt University PAVE
VU Station B 351736
Nashville, TN 37235-1736

Phone: 615-322-7827

Fax: 615-322-3297

E-mail: pave@vanderbilt.edu

Website: https://pave.vanderbilt.edu

Program Type: Math, Sciences, Engineering, and Computer Science/Technology

Grade/Age Levels: Grades 11–12

Description: PAVE is a 5-week summer course of study designed to strengthen the academic skills of students who are planning to enter a college engineering, premedical, science, or technology program. The program introduces students to college life while improving their problem-solving, technical writing, computer, and laboratory skills.

Aquatic Sciences Adventure Camp

Contact: Aaron Swink, Assistant Director for Education

Address: Aquatic Science Adventure Camp
Edwards Aquifer Research and Data Center
Texas State University
601 University Dr.
San Marcos, TX 78666

Phone: 512-245-2329

Fax: 512-245-2669

E-mail: aps36@txstate.edu

Website: http://www.eardc.txstate.edu/camp.html

Program Type: Academic Enrichment

Grade/Age Levels: Ages 9–15

Description: Aquatic Sciences Adventure Camp is a fun camp for students who are interested in aquatic or marine sciences. The program includes a mixture of educational and recreational activities, including aquatic biology and water chemistry, swimming, tubing, scuba/snorkeling, river rafting, a glass-bottom boat ride, a Sea World trip, and more. The residential coeducational camp is conducted during weekly sessions in June and July.

AwesomeMath Summer Program

Contact: Dr. Titu Andreescu

Address: AwesomeMath Summer Program
c/o Dr. Titu Andreescu
3425 Neiman Rd.
Plano, TX 75025

Phone: 702-RAD-MATH

E-mail: tandreescu@gmail.com

Website: http://www.awesomemath.org/summer-program

Program Type: Math, Sciences, Engineering, and Computer Science/Technology

Grade/Age Levels: Grades 6–11

Description: The AwesomeMath Summer Program is a 3-week residential camp designed to hone middle school and high school students' mathematical problem-solving skills up to the Olympiad level. Each student takes two courses of his or her choice meant to increase problem-solving skills. Recreational activities are also provided. Visit the website for current dates and locations.

Baylor University Summer Science Research Program (BUSSRP)

Contact: Ms. Carol McCulloch, Assistant to the Associate Deans, or Dr. Frank Mathis, Director and Associate Dean for Sciences

Address: BUSSRP
One Bear Place #97344
Waco, TX 76798

Phone: 254-710-4288

Fax: 254-710-1628

E-mail: BUSSRP@baylor.edu

Website: http://www.baylor.edu/summerscience

Program Type: Math, Sciences, Engineering, and Computer Science/Technology

Grade/Age Levels: Rising grade 13

Description: The purpose of the Baylor University Summer Science Research Program (BUSSRP) is to give superior students hands-on research experience by working on research projects with Baylor University science professors in many disciplines. The research program occurs during the university's second session of summer school.

Students are selected from incoming Baylor freshmen to be involved in this summer research program, which allows them to earn one semester hour of college credit. It is hoped that this experience will have a positive effect on student interest in careers in science disciplines and allow them to begin a program of undergraduate research.

Camp on the Coast Summer Theatre Workshop

Contact: Mr. Kelly Russell

Address: Camp on the Coast
Texas A&M University at Corpus Christi
6300 Ocean Dr., Unit 5724
Corpus Christi, TX 78412

Phone: 361-825-2316

E-mail: Kelly.Russell@tamucc.edu

Website: http://cla.tamucc.edu/theatre/events/camp.html

Program Type: Fine, Performing, and Visual Arts

Grade/Age Levels: Grades 9–12

Description: The Texas A&M University at Corpus Christi Summer Theatre Workshop is a 2-week residential camp designed for high school students seeking a highly intensive and creative theatre experience. Participants will rehearse and perform in a one-act play directed by one of five highly successful theatre educators. Students will also study acting, voice, and movement in morning classes taught by TAMU-CC Theatre faculty.

CATS SummerStars Musical Theatre Intensive Camp

Address: SummerStars Musical
Theatre Intensive Camp
Creative Arts Theatre and School
602 E. South St.
Arlington, TX 76010

Phone: 817-861-2287

Website: http://creativearts.org

Program Type: Fine, Performing, and Visual Arts

Grade/Age Levels: Rising grades 7–12

Description: SummerStars is a 2-week comprehensive residential and commuter program for teens. Taught by professional actors, directors, choreographers, and musicians, the program encompasses many aspects of a theatrical production, focusing on acting, singing, and dancing. Mornings of the program find the students rotating among classes in acting techniques, music, and dance. Afternoons are devoted to rehearsals, as this program concludes with a full musical production. If you are looking for an intense and true summer stock experience, consider CATS this summer.

Clark Scholars Program at Texas Tech University

Contact: Dr. Michael San Francisco, Director

Address: Clark Scholars Program
Texas Tech University
Box 43131
Lubbock, TX 79409-3131

Phone: 806-742-1828

Fax: 806-742-2047

E-mail: michael.sanfrancisco@ttu.edu

Website: http://www.clarkscholars.ttu.edu

Program Type: Academic Enrichment

Grade/Age Levels: Ages 17 and up

Description: The Clark Scholars Program is an intensive 7-week summer research program for highly qualified high school juniors and seniors. The scholars will receive a $750 tax-free stipend and room and board. Students work with university faculty in research areas including but not limited to biological sciences, chemistry and biochemistry, mathematics, all areas of engineering, human sciences, agricultural sciences, psychology, the arts, humanities, social sciences, and human health (cancer, cell biology, microbiology, etc.).

Creative Writing Camp

Contact:	Mr. Jack McBride, Program Director
Address:	Creative Writing Camp Co-sponsored by Writers in the Schools and Rice University's School Literacy & Culture 1523 W. Main Houston, TX 77006
Phone:	713-523-3877
Fax:	866-793-4865 (toll-free)
E-mail:	mail@witshouston.org
Website:	http://www.witshouston.org
Program Type:	Academic Enrichment
Grade/Age Levels:	Grades K–12
Description:	Creative Writing Camp offers a supportive environment where children engage in writing stories, poetry, essays, and plays, as well as simply reading for pleasure. Through these activities, even the most hesitant child discovers the joy in writing, the intrigue of language, and the confidence of authorship. Students will work with teachers and writers, and the low teacher-student ratios ensure individual attention. Workshops end with a culminating performance and/or reading, and each child will receive an anthology with his or her published work.

Institute for the Development and Enrichment of Advanced Learners (IDEAL) at Texas Tech University

Contact: Isaac Flores, Assistant Director

Address: Institute for the Development and Enrichment of Advanced Learners
Texas Tech University
Box 41008
Lubbock, TX 79409-1008

Phone: 806-742-2420

Fax: 806-742-2396

E-mail: ideal@ttu.edu

Website: http://www.ideal.ttu.edu

Program Type: Academic Enrichment; Math, Sciences, Engineering, and Computer Science/Technology; Fine, Performing, and Visual Arts; Leadership/Service/Volunteer

Grade/Age Levels: Grades K–12

Description: IDEAL offers academic enrichment programs to students in grades K–12 to promote academic excellence, citizenship, leadership, diversity, and appreciation of the arts. Programs include:

- Super Saturdays
- Shake Hands With Your Future
- Science: It's a Girl Thing
- Run on the Wind
- Video Game Design

Lone Star Leadership Academy

Contact:	Ms. Ashley Barnes, Admissions Director
Address:	Education in Action P.O. Box 2285 Keller, TX 76244
Phone:	817-562-4957
Fax:	817-562-2058
E-mail:	admissions@educationinaction.org
Website:	http://www.educationinaction.org
Program Type:	Leadership/Service/Volunteer
Grade/Age Levels:	Grades 4–8
Description:	Lone Star Leadership Academies are Sunday–Friday residential leadership development camps for outstanding fourth–eighth graders. Participants travel to Dallas/Fort Worth, Austin/San Antonio, or Houston/Galveston to develop leadership skills while learning about the great state of Texas through visits to numerous significant Texas sites with Texas educators. Participants learn about unique careers and add to their academic résumés.

Longhorn Music Camp

Address: Longhorn Music Camp
The University of Texas at Austin
1 University Station E3100
Austin, TX 78712

Phone: 512-232-2080

Fax: 512-232-3907

E-mail: lmc@austin.utexas.edu

Website: http://lmc.music.utexas.edu

Program Type: Fine, Performing, and Visual Arts

Grade/Age Levels: Grades 6–12

Description: Longhorn Music Camp provides summer music programs for students completing grades 6–12 in band, orchestra, choir, harp, and piano (disciplines vary by grade). This program includes both residential and commuter options. Some of the programs require auditions.

SMU College Experience

Address:	SMU College Experience Program P.O. Box 750383 Dallas, TX 75275-0383
Phone:	214-768-0123
Fax:	214-768-3147
E-mail:	gifted@smu.edu
Website:	http://www.smu.edu/ce
Program Type:	Academic Enrichment
Grade/Age Levels:	Rising grades 11–12
Description:	Academically talented high school students can get a head start on college and a taste of campus life during this exciting 5-week summer program at SMU. The selection of college-credit subjects for morning classes includes philosophy, English, math, psychology, history, and government. In the afternoon, all College Experience students will participate in a "core" class or humanities overview class for 3 hours of college credit. Students who elect to live in the CE residence hall will participate in special cultural, educational, and recreational activities.

SMU Talented and Gifted Program

Contact: Ms. Marilyn Swanson, Director of Programming

Address: Southern Methodist University
Gifted Students Institute Talented and Gifted Program
P.O. Box 750383
Dallas, TX 75275-0383

Phone: 214-768-0123

Fax: 214-768-3147

E-mail: gifted@smu.edu

Website: http://www.smu.edu/tag

Program Type: Academic Enrichment

Grade/Age Levels: Rising grades 8–10

Description: During this 3-week residential program, students participate in two stimulating classes chosen from a wide selection of SMU credit and noncredit courses. Cultural enrichment activities are provided for all TAG students. Three-hour credit courses include leadership, mathematical sciences, political science, mechanical engineering, psychology, philosophy, and ethics. Noncredit courses include writing, engineering, theater arts, public discourse, mathematics, music, photography, physics, geography, and rocketry. Enrollment is limited to 80 students. Participants are selected on the basis of academic ability and motivation as demonstrated by grades, SAT or ACT scores, teacher recommendations, and other application requirements.

Summer Academy in Architecture

Address: Summer Academy in Architecture
The University of Texas at Austin
1 University Station–B7500
Austin, TX 78712-0222

Phone: 512-471-8909

Fax: 512-471-7033

E-mail: academy@austin.utexas.edu

Website: http://soa.utexas.edu/summeracademy

Program Type: Academic Enrichment; Fine, Performing, and Visual Arts

Grade/Age Levels: Ages 17 and up

Description: The Summer Academy is an intensive 4-week introductory course in architecture that assumes no prior study in the field, but a great familiarity with it through the experience of occupying places. Through a series of individual design projects, the Academy introduces students to many of the important aspects of architecture and encourages personal exploration.

Academy students are provided individual studio space in which to work for the summer session. The studio environment of the Academy provides individual attention through daily tutorials and group discussions with an average student-to-teacher ratio of 10:1. Particular attention is paid to developing skills in drawing and model construction. Daily studio assignments encompass ideas that span the breadth of architectural practice and theory, such as structure, materials, site, light, view, context, and experience. Individual studio work is supplemented by a series of supporting activities and events

Description, Continued

that include faculty and visiting lectures, a film series, site visits, class reviews, and periodic meetings that emphasize students' more practical concerns (i.e., application procedures, general admissions policies, and the preparation of a portfolio or résumé).

Summer Strings Music Camp

Contact: Mr. Royce Coatney

Address: Royce and Sylvia Coatney
Summer Strings Camp Program Directors
UTA Box 19105
Arlington, TX 76019

Phone: 817-469-1393

E-mail: utasummerstringscamp@gmail.com

Website: http://arlingtonsummerstrings.org

Program Type: Fine, Performing, and Visual Arts

Grade/Age Levels: Grades 6–12

Description: This annual program provides young string players an opportunity to improve their musical skills and develop new friendships with students from around the state. Students participate in daily rehearsals, sectionals, and classes in music theory, music history, and conducting. All-State Master Classes are available for high school students. All students audition for placement in one of six orchestras.

Texas A&M University at Galveston TAG

TEXAS

Contact: Ms. Daisy Dailey, Director

Address: Texas A&M University at Galveston
TAG
P.O. Box 1675
Galveston, TX 77553

Phone: 409-740-4525

Fax: 409-470-4894

E-mail: daileyd@tamug.edu

Website: http://www.tamug.edu/seacamp

Program Type: Math, Sciences, Engineering, and Computer Science/Technology

Grade/Age Levels: Ages 14–18

Description: TAG, a residential summer program for high ability students ages 14–18, is offered at Texas A&M University at Galveston. These career-oriented courses will help students expand their horizons with a preparatory course in the field of their choice: veterinary medicine, marine engineering, premedicine, marine biology research, or marine science research.

Texas Brigades Wildlife Education and Leadership Development Camps

Contact: Ms. Helen Holdsworth, Executive Director

Phone: 210-556-1391; 855-892-7447

Fax: 210-826-4933

E-mail: hholdsworth@texas-wildlife.org

Website: http://www.texasbrigades.org

Program Type: Leadership/Service/Volunteer

Grade/Age Levels: Ages 13–17

Description: The Texas Brigades is a wildlife-focused program for students. The Texas Brigades' mission is to educate and empower youth with leadership skills and knowledge in wildlife, fisheries, and land stewardship to become conservation ambassadors for a sustained natural resource legacy. There are five different camps: Bobwhite Brigade, Buckskin Brigade, Bass Brigade, Ranch Brigade, and Waterfowl Brigade. Each 4 1/2-day camp is instructed by top wildlife professionals and resource managers.

Texas Governor's School

Contact: Dr. Dorothy Sisk

Address: Texas Governor's School
Lamar University
P.O. Box 10034
Beaumont, TX 77710

Phone: 409-880-8046

Fax: 409-880-8384

E-mail: dorothy.sisk@lamar.edu

Website: http://education.lamar.edu/texas-governors-school

Program Type: Academic Enrichment

Grade/Age Levels: Grades 11 and up

Description: The Texas Governor's School is a summer residential program at Lamar University in Beaumont, TX, that provides innovative academics for gifted adolescents (finishing their sophomore year). The 3-week program offers courses not usually provided in high school that emphasize hands-on activities designed to help students develop their leadership and ethical decision-making skills. Students actively participate in cognitively challenging tasks that build on their ability to think, reflect, and experience success. Evening seminars are provided with individuals who have demonstrated leadership at the state, national, and international levels. Students host these sessions and engage in lively Q&A with eminent leaders in business, sciences, and the arts.

Texas State University Honors Summer Math Camp

Contact: Dr. Max Warshauer, Director

Address: Texas State University
Honors Summer Math Camp
Texas Mathworks
601 University Dr.
San Marcos, TX 78666

Phone: 512-245-3439

Fax: 512-245-1469

E-mail: mathworks@txstate.edu

Website: http://www.txstate.edu/mathworks/camps/hsmc.html

Program Type: Academic Enrichment; Math, Sciences, Engineering, and Computer Science/Technology

Grade/Age Levels: Grades 10–12

Description: The goal of the Texas State Honors Summer Math Camp is to excite talented young students about doing mathematics, to teach students to reason rigorously and precisely, and to develop questioning minds. The focus on number theory is modeled after the Ross Summer Program at Ohio State, teaching students to "think deeply of simple things" (Arnold Ross). Students work together exploring ideas and share in the excitement of finding the simple mathematical ideas that underline and explain seemingly complex problems. First-year students take courses in elementary number theory, mathematical computer programming, and an honors seminar. Returning students study combinatorics, analysis, and selected short courses. Advanced students may also work on a supervised Siemens Competition research project.

Texas State University Junior Summer Math Camp

Contact: Mr. Max Warshauer, Director

Address: Texas State University
Junior Summer Math Camp
601 University Dr.
San Marcos, TX 78666

Phone: 512-245-3439

Fax: 512-245-1469

E-mail: mathworks@txstate.edu

Website: http://www.txstate.edu/mathworks/camps/jsmc.html

Program Type: Math, Sciences, Engineering, and Computer Science/Technology; Academic Enrichment

Grade/Age Levels: Rising grades 4–8

Description: The Texas State Junior Summer Math Camp is a nationally recognized math program for students in grades 4–8. There are five levels in the program. Level 1, the Mathematical Mystery Tour, is for students in grades 4–5. It introduces students to the basic ideas in algebra through the use of children's drama and activities. Level 2, MathQuest, is for students in grades 5–6, and it introduces students to functions, fractions, decimals, and using a graphing calculator. Level 3, Math Explorations, is for students in grades 6–7. This level introduces algebraic concepts motivated by geometry. Levels 1–3 prepare students to study algebra, while introducing students to the excitement of doing math together. In Level 4, Combinatorics, students study basic counting principals and discrete math, which are topics often overlooked in the standard school curriculum. Level 5 includes a special residential training program for top students throughout Texas.

University for Young People at Baylor

Contact: Dr. Mary M. Witte, Director

Address: University for Young People
Baylor University
Center for Community Learning
and Enrichment
One Bear Place #97282
Waco, TX 76798

Phone: 254-710-2171

Fax: 254-710-4904

E-mail: CenterSupport@baylor.edu

Website: http://www.baylor.edu/SOE/CCLE

Program Type: Academic Enrichment

Grade/Age Levels: Grades 1–12

Description: University for Young People is a summer enrichment program for rising first graders through rising 12th graders. Younger students meet at an elementary school to study an interdisciplinary theme such as Structures, where they discover the many structures that are involved in building a new city. Older students attend classes on the Baylor campus in the sciences, social sciences, fine arts, and technology.

USA Chess
National Summer Chess Camp Tour

Contact: Mr. Mike Borchelt

Address: USA Chess
National Summer Chess Camp Tour
18911 Forest Bend Creek Way
Spring, TX 77379

Phone: 888-652-4377; 281-257-0078

Website: http://www.usachess.com/camcategory.php?cpid=1

Program Type: Academic Enrichment

Grade/Age Levels: Ages 5–15

Description: USA Chess provides chess activities for children in more than 80 U.S. cities. Activities include a national summer chess camp tour, scholastic tournaments, school chess programs, and private/group lessons.

Young Authors' Writing Camp/ Writers' Island Workshop

Contact: Ms. Catherine Quick, Camp Director

Address: Young Authors Writing Camp
Texas A&M University-Corpus Christi
6300 Ocean Dr., Unit 5813
Corpus Christi, TX 78412

Phone: 361-825-3025

E-mail: catherine.quick@tamucc.edu

Website: http://cbwp.tamucc.edu/YA%20Camp%20index.html

Program Type: Academic Enrichment

Grade/Age Levels: Grades 3–12

Description: The Young Authors' Writing Camp is designed to provide elementary and middle school students/authors with opportunities to expand their interest in writing and to experience writing as a fun and creative opportunity for self-expression and communication with others. The camp includes a variety of writing activities, visits with poets and artists, and nature walks. The camp staff consists of a team of university professors, elementary school teachers, and university students.

The Writers' Island Workshop is designed to provide high school writers with opportunities to expand their interest in writing and to experience a professional style writer's workshop. The workshop includes a variety of writing activities, as well as visits with poets and artists and nature walks. The camp staff consists of a team of university professors, high school teachers, and university students.

Zoo Careers Camp

Address: Zoo Careers Camp
Fort Worth Zoo
1989 Colonial Parkway
Fort Worth, TX 76110

Phone: 817-759-7200

Fax: 817-759-7201

E-mail: education@fortworthzoo.org

Website: http://www.fortworthzoo.org/education/camps-programs/zoo-careers-camp

Program Type: Academic Enrichment

Grade/Age Levels: Rising grades 9–12

Description: Zoo Careers Camp is designed for high school students entering grades 9–12 who are interested in zoological sciences, wildlife conservation and animal-related careers. During this 5-day overnight camp, participants will learn about animal care, husbandry, maintenance, training, and accompany animal staff on daily schedules, participate in animal care activities, and attend presentations given by zoo staff.

University of Utah Summer Mathematics Program for High School Students

UTAH

Contact: Ms. Aryn DeJulis, Director of Undergraduate Services

Address: University of Utah
Department of Mathematics
155 South 1400 East, JWB 233
Salt Lake City, UT 84112-0090

Phone: 801-581-6851; 801-585-9478

Fax: 801-581-4148

E-mail: dejulis@math.utah.edu

Website: http://www.math.utah.edu/hsp

Program Type: Math, Sciences, Engineering, and Computer Science/Technology

Grade/Age Levels: Grades 9–12

Description: The Summer Mathematics Program for High School Students at the University of Utah provides outstanding students an opportunity to develop their talents to the fullest. By presenting intriguing puzzles, challenging problems, and powerful ideas, the program stimulates curiosity, develops the intellect, and lays a strong foundation for future work in mathematics, the sciences, or science-related careers. In completing this 3-week program, participants will receive three university credits in mathematics. The prerequisite for the program is precalculus. Calculus is not required. Preference will be given to students between their junior and senior years.

University of Utah High School University Program (HSUP)

Address: University of Utah
Student Recruitment HSUP
200 S. Central Campus Dr., Rm. 80
Salt Lake City, UT 84112

Phone: 801-585-6718

Website: http://admissions.utah.edu/academics/hsup.php

Program Type: Academic Enrichment

Grade/Age Levels: Grades 10–12

Description: High School University Program is for high school sophomores through seniors who want to take college-level course work not available at the high school; or for students who want to get a head start on a college career. Students in this program are generating an official university transcript and completed courses are applied toward university credit. Students may participate in any of the 1000 and 2000 series classes the university is currently offering, with the exception of online/telecourses, as long as they meet the prerequisites.

The University of Utah also offers an array of programs during the summer in its Continuing Education program. For a complete listing, visit http://www.smartkids.utah.edu.

Future Leader Camp

Address: Future Leader Camp
Norwich University
27 I.D. White Ave.
Northfield, VT 05663

Phone: 802-485-2531

Fax: 802-485-2739

E-mail: flc@norwich.edu

Website: http://www.norwich.edu/admissions/summerprograms/flc

Program Type: Leadership/Service/Volunteer

Grade/Age Levels: Rising grades 10 and up

Description: The Future Leader Camp (FLC) is a 2-week summer program dedicated to developing the leadership potential of current high school students. FLC provides participants with a challenging and meaningful adventure camp experience while building an understanding of small-group leadership techniques, leadership ethics, teamwork, problem solving, and effective communication.

Middlebury-Monterey Language Academy

Contact: Mimi Clark

Address: Middlebury-Monterey Language Academy
23 Pond Ln.
Middlebury, VT 05753

Phone: 888-216-0135

E-mail: mmla.info@middleburyinteractive.com

Website: http://mmla.middlebury.edu/

Program Type: Foreign Language

Grade/Age Levels: Rising grades 8 and up

Description: Middlebury-Monterey Language Academy (MMLA) offers immersive residential summer language programs in the U.S. and abroad in Arabic, Chinese, French, German, and Spanish and attracts students in grades 8–12. At the Academy, students take the Language Pledge®, which is a formal commitment to communicate exclusively in the language of study, creating a total language-immersion environment where students gain up to a year of language acquisition in only 4 weeks on campus.

UVM-GIV Engineering Summer Institute

E-mail: giv@sover.net

Website: http://www.uvm.edu/~cems/giv

Program Type: Math, Sciences, Engineering, and Computer Science/Technology; Academic Enrichment

Grade/Age Levels: Rising grades 9 and up

Description: Challenge yourself to think outside the box with a hands-on project, laboratory experiences, faculty presentations, and enlightening tours. You'll learn how technology impacts the human experience. Experience the thrill of creating sand arches at the beach and become part of an innovative team to work on one of the following diversified projects that will stretch your brain: Bio Mass Conversion, Wind Energy Conversion Systems, Robotics Technology, or Aeronautical Engineering. Students will be housed in campus dorms and will explore career opportunities and develop firsthand awareness of the nature of college life.

Northern Virginia Writing Project Student Summer Institute

Contact:	Ms. Cathy Hailey, Co-Director
Address:	Northern Virginia Writing Project Student Summer Institute George Mason University MS 3E4 4400 University Drive Fairfax, VA 22030-4444
Phone:	571-206-4987
E-mail:	youngwriters@nvwp.org
Website:	http://www.nvwp.org/youngwriters/ssi
Program Type:	Academic Enrichment
Grade/Age Levels:	Grades 5–12
Description:	The Northern Virginia Writing Project Student Summer Institute is an annual 2-week writing enrichment program for approximately 120 selected students from grades 5–12. The young writers come to the George Mason University campus in Fairfax, VA, to work with writing teachers and consultants. The writing produced in the Institute is published in an anthology and celebrated as a culminating event of the Institute.

Pre-Collegiate Summer Program in Early American History

Contact:	Dr. Carolyn Whittenburg, Director
Address:	Pre-Collegiate Summer Program in Early American History William & Mary National Institute of American History and Democracy P.O. Box 8795 Williamsburg, VA 23187-8795
Phone:	757-221-7652
E-mail:	precol@wm.edu
Website:	http://www.wm.edu/as/niahd/ precollegiatesummer
Program Type:	Academic Enrichment
Grade/Age Levels:	Rising grades 11 and up
Description:	The National Institute of American History and Democracy (NIAHD) is a partnership between William & Mary and the Colonial Williamsburg Foundation. It is dedicated to the study of the American past, material culture, and museums. The Institute sponsors The Pre-Collegiate Summer Program in Early American History, which includes 4 hours of academic credit. The program allows for students to experience a high degree of interaction with researchers in early American history. Students take daily field trips to study "on site" at the excellent historic locations, museums, and archaeological sites in eastern Virginia. They participate in afternoon discussion seminars and enjoy special evening programs that include speakers, music, dance, and costumed interpreters. Students may also join in optional archaeological digs on weekends.

Research Science Institute (RSI)

Contact: Ms. Maite Ballestero,
Vice President, Programs

Address: Research Science Institute
Massachusetts Institute of Technology
Center for Excellence in Education
8201 Greensboro Dr., Ste. 215
McLean, VA 22102

Phone: 703-448-9662

Fax: 703-448-9068

E-mail: cee@cee.org; rsi@cee.org

Website: http://www.cee.org/research-science-institute

Program Type: Math, Sciences, Engineering, and Computer Science/Technology; Academic Enrichment; Internships/Paid Positions

Grade/Age Levels: Grade 11

Description: Research Science Institute (RSI) is an intense summer program in which some of the most talented high school students from the U.S. and around the world come together to do cutting-edge science and mathematics research. Living on the MIT campus, they do research projects under the guidance of mentors from the university and area institutions and corporations. RSI is open to students who have completed the third year of high school, or the equivalent. Program application deadline is early January.

Student Conservation Association

Address: Student Conservation Association
4245 North Fairfax Drive
Suite 825
Arlington, VA 22203

Phone: 703-524-2441

Fax: 703-524-2451

E-mail: SCArecruiting@thesca.org

Website: http://www.thesca.org

Program Type: Internships/Paid Positions; Leadership/Service/Volunteer

Grade/Age Levels: Rising grades 10 and up

Description: With a mission to create the next generation of conservation leaders through hands-on stewardship of the environment, the Student Conservation Association (SCA) is the nation's largest and oldest provider of conservation service opportunities. SCA creates hands-on experiences that transform both lives and lands, empowering young people from diverse backgrounds to plan, act, and lead while they ensure America's natural legacy. More than 4,000 SCA members complete close to 2 million hours of conservation service annually.

SCA offers 3–12–month expenses-paid internships for those 18 and older. Students ages 15–19 can take part in SCA's Conservation Crews.

Work with natural, cultural resource management agencies (e.g., National Park Service, U.S. Forest Service) and be part of a team of 6–8 students that spends a month on a conservation assignment during summer school vacation.

University of Virginia (UVA) Saturday and Summer Enrichment Program

Contact:	Julie Baird, Director
Address:	Saturday and Summer Enrichment Program University of Virginia P.O. Box 400264 Charlottesville, VA 22904-4264
Phone:	434-924-3182
Fax:	434-982-2008
E-mail:	curry-sep@virginia.edu
Website:	http://curry.virginia.edu/sep
Program Type:	Academic Enrichment
Grade/Age Levels:	Grades 5–11
Description:	UVA's Summer Enrichment Program provides extended study in liberal arts, social science, math, science, and technology. Cost includes tuition, room and board, and all materials. Need-based scholarships are available.

University of Virginia Summer Language Institute

Address: Summer Language Institute
University of Virginia
P.O. Box 400161
Charlottesville, VA 22904-4161

Phone: 434-924-3371

Fax: 434-924-1483

E-mail: uvasli@virginia.edu

Website: http://www.virginia.edu/summer/SLI

Program Type: Foreign Language

Grade/Age Levels: Rising grades 11–12

Description: The University of Virginia's Summer Language Institute offers 8-week programs in Arabic, French, German, Hebrew, Italian, Latin, Russian, Spanish, Tibetan, and Chinese in a near-immersion environment. These 10 programs are designed to serve people who wish to attain an intermediate level of competence in a new language in just one summer. Students who successfully complete the program earn 12 credits, the equivalent of 2 academic years of language study at the college level. The exceptions are the Arabic and Chinese programs, which offer eight credits or the equivalent of one academic year of study at either the elementary or intermediate level. Participants attend classes 5 days a week, up to 7.5 hours a day. The limited class size allows for individualized and group instruction not usually available in standard language classrooms. Please note that students under the age of 18 are not eligible to live in university housing.

University of Virginia Young Writers Workshop

Contact: Ms. Margo Figgins, Director

Address: Young Writers Workshop
The University of Virginia
The Curry School
P.O. Box 400273
Charlottesville, VA 22903

Phone: 434-924-0836

Fax: 434-924-0747

E-mail: writers@virginia.edu

Website: http://theyoungwriters.org

Program Type: Academic Enrichment; Fine, Performing, and Visual Arts

Grade/Age Levels: Rising grades 9–12

Description: The Young Writers Workshop of the University of Virginia, established in 1982, brings together a community of writers with a common purpose: to create a supportive and noncompetitive environment where teenagers can live and work as artists. Every staff member has a commitment to writing. The faculty, professional authors interested in developing new talent, brings practical experience to the workshop setting.

Virginia Association of Soil and Water Conservation Youth Conservation Camp

Contact:	Ms. Elizabeth Sokolik
Address:	Virginia Association of Soil and Water Conservation Districts Youth Conservation Camp 7308 Hanover Green Dr., Ste. 100 Mechanicsville, VA 23111
Phone:	804-559-0324
Fax:	804-559-0325
E-mail:	elizabeth.sokolik@vaswcd.org
Website:	http://vaswcd.org/conservation-camp
Program Type:	Math, Sciences, Engineering, and Computer Science/Technology
Grade/Age Levels:	Grades 9–12
Description:	For more than 30 years, the Virginia Association of Soil and Water Conservation Districts has sponsored a weeklong summer conservation camp for Virginia high school students on the campus of Virginia Tech. The program brings together about 70 interested students for a week of learning about Virginia's natural resources from conservation professionals and faculty from Virginia Tech. Most of the instruction is hands-on and outdoors.

Salish Summer Sailing and Science Expeditions

Contact: Eric Strickler, Program Manager

Address: Salish Summer Sailing and Science Expeditions
Salish Sea Expeditions
1257 Patmos Ln. NW
Bainbridge Island, WA 98110

Phone: 206-780-7848

Fax: 206-780-9005

E-mail: eric@salish.org

Website: http://www.salish.org

Program Type: Math, Sciences, Engineering, and Computer Science/Technology

Grade/Age Levels: Ages 10–14

Description: Salish Sea Expeditions was formed in 1994 after much consulting with teachers and administrators about the need for a program to give middle and high school students the opportunity to do real hands-on science through student-designed and driven research opportunities. Following inquiry-based methodologies, students are given control and ownership of many aspects of their Salish learning experience, with the belief that students would develop a joy for learning and a newfound appreciation for science that they would carry back to their traditional classroom settings. Programs are organized at our small headquarters on Bainbridge Island, and occur throughout Puget Sound during the school year on our sailing research vessel the s/v *Carlyn*. During summer months, we utilize the same educational philosophy to inspire campers to pursue science in many locations around Puget Sound. Salish's growing success is a result of the commitment to a

Description, Continued novel idea by an inspired group of staff, board members, volunteers, donors, and others who believed in the creation of an unparalleled learning experience.

Summer Institute for Mathematics at the University of Washington (SIMUW)

Address: SIMUW
Department of Mathematics
University of Washington
Box 354350
Seattle, WA 98195-4350

Phone: 305-707-4689

Fax: 206-543-0397

E-mail: simuw@math.washington.edu

Website: http://www.simuw.net

Program Type: Math, Sciences, Engineering, Computer Science, and Technology

Grade/Age Levels: Rising grades 10–12

Description: SIMUW provides a carefully selected group of motivated high school students with ample opportunities to acquire a full appreciation of the nature of mathematics: its wide-ranging content, the intrinsic beauty of its ideas, the nature of mathematical argument and rigorous proof, the surprising power of mathematics within the sciences and beyond.

The program includes six intensive 2-week courses taught by university professors on topics that change from year to year. In the past, students have studied methods of argument, combinatorics, hyperbolic geometry, game theory, group theory, coding theory, and much more. In addition, there are 12 guest lectures on a wide variety of subjects and in many different formats, allowing students to glimpse even more mathematical areas, as well as participate in hands-on mathematical

Description, Continued

activities. When not in class, students work on problems in groups or individually, have mathematical discussions with the Teaching Assistant Counselors, and participate in social events, sports, and weekly Saturday outings. They develop many new interests and close friendships, the end of the program coming way too soon.

To be eligible for admission to SIMUW, students must be residents of Washington, British Columbia, Oregon, Idaho, or Alaska, and have completed 3 years of high school mathematics, including algebra, geometry, and trigonometry.

Wesleyan Summer Gifted Program

Contact: Dr. Eric Waggoner, Director

Address: West Virginia Wesleyan College
Box 122
Buckhannon, WV 26201

Phone: 304-473-8072

Fax: 304-472-2571

E-mail: sgp@wvwc.edu

Website: http://www.wvwc.edu/summergifted

Program Type: Academic Enrichment

Grade/Age Levels: Grades 5–12

Description: The Summer Gifted Program at West Virginia Wesleyan College in Buckhannon, WV, is a terrific experience for gifted and talented youth in grades 5–12. Founded in 1983 by a college physics professor who had gifted children of his own, the camp is a 2-week, overnight experience, the only program of its kind in the region, and the most affordable gifted camp in the country. Students get a taste of college and life in the dorms as they attend advanced classes taught by college professors and surrounded by children who possess similar abilities and interests. Wesleyan's campus has all the major recreational facilities you would expect: basketball courts, an indoor swimming pool, racquetball courts, an outdoor track, tennis courts, and soccer fields. Activities, games, guest speakers, demonstrations, field trips, and a talent show foster students' social skills and creativity. The camp is small, with a low student-teacher ratio. Many students return year after year.

Archaeology Public Field School

Contact:	Jean Dowiasch, Education Coordinator
Address:	Archaeology Public Field School University of Wisconsin-La Crosse Mississippi Valley Archeology Center 1725 State St. La Crosse, WI 54601
Phone:	608-785-8454
Fax:	608-785-6474
E-mail:	jdowiasch@uwlax.edu
Website:	http://mrac/uwlax.edu
Program Type:	Academic Enrichment
Grade/Age Levels:	Grades 9–12
Description:	Students participate in an actual archaeological excavation by working alongside professional archaeologists in the field. Campers take part in small-scale excavations (test units) and survey work. Lab work may include washing ceramics, stone tools, and other remains, and sorting them into basic categories. No previous experience is necessary.

Milwaukee School of Engineering Summer Programs

Contact: Codi Alger

Address: MSOE Summer Programs
Milwaukee School of Engineering
1025 N. Broadway
Milwaukee, WI 53202-3109

Phone: 800-332-6763

E-mail: summerprograms@msoe.edu

Website: http://www.msoe.edu/summer

Program Type: Academic Enrichment

Grade/Age Levels: Grades 10–12

Description: This weeklong summer camp will challenge you to learn more about a specific career field: architectural engineering/building construction; biomedical engineering; computer engineering/software engineering; electrical engineering; mechanical engineering/industrial engineering/nursing; business; or technical communication. You will get hands-on exposure by working in our labs on exciting projects. Working closely with MSOE faculty and current students is an integral part of the program.

University of Wisconsin-Milwaukee Architecture Summer Camp

Contact: Ms. Tammy Taylor, Associate Director

Address: Architecture Summer Camp
University of Wisconsin-Milwaukee
School of Architecture and Urban Planning
P.O. Box 413
Milwaukee, WI 53201-0413

Phone: 414-229-5821; 414-229-4015

Fax: 414-229-6976

E-mail: ttaylor@uwm.edu

Website: http://www4.uwm.edu/sarup/admissions/outreach/summercamp/summercamp.cfm

Program Type: Academic Enrichment

Grade/Age Levels: Grades 9–12

Description: The School of Architecture and Urban Planning (SARUP) Architecture Summer Camp is a weeklong educational program for exceptionally motivated high school students (grades 9–12) contemplating the study of architecture at the university level. Students live in the residence halls at the University of Wisconsin-Milwaukee to get a true taste of college life.

The week's activities are anchored by the design studio, in which students develop three projects that address the fundamental issues of space making in architecture. The projects introduce students to the creation and manipulation of space that is at the center of architectural practice.

Wisconsin Center for Academically Talented Youth (WCATY) Summer Programs

Contact: Ola Skyba, Summer Program Director

Address: Wisconsin Center for Academically Talented Youth
University of Wisconsin-Madison
Teacher Education Building
225 N Mills St., Ste. 264
Madison, WI 53706

Phone: 608-890-3260

Fax: 608-265-4309

E-mail: wcaty@education.wisc.edu

Website: http://wcatyeop.wcatyweb.org

Program Type: Academic Enrichment; Math, Sciences, Engineering, and Computer Science/Technology; Fine, Performing, and Visual Arts

Grade/Age Levels: Grades 3–12

Description: WCATY offers several programs for talented children and youth, including:

» *Accelerated Learning Program* (ALP) for grades 9–12; UW-Madison campus;

» *Summer Transitional Enrichment Program* (STEP) for grades 7–8; UW-Madison campus; and

» *Young Students Summer Program* (YSSP) for grades 4–6; Beloit College.

Teton Science Schools

Address: Teton Science Schools
700 Coyote Canyon Rd.
Jackson, WY 83001

Phone: 307-733-1313

Fax: 307-733-7560

E-mail: info@tetonscience.org

Website: http://www.tetonscience.org

Program Type: Math, Sciences, Engineering, and Computer Science/Technology

Grade/Age Levels: Grades K–12

Description: Join students from around the country on an educational adventure exploring field research, natural history, and backcountry experiences in the Greater Yellowstone Ecosystem. Teton Science Schools hosts summer camps for a variety of age groups, including:

» Jackson Hole Science Camps, grades K–9;
» High School Summer Camps, grades 9–12; and
» Journeys School Summer Innovation Academy, grades 3–8.

University of Wyoming Engineering Summer Program

Address: Engineering Summer Program
University of Wyoming
College of Engineering
Dept. 3295
1000 E. University Ave.
Laramie, WY 82071

Phone: 307-766-3180

E-mail: esp@uwyo.edu

Website: http://www.uwyo.edu/ceas/studentservices/high-school/esp

Program Type: Math, Sciences, Engineering, and Computer Science/Technology

Grade/Age Levels: Grade 11

Description: The College of Engineering and Applied Science, UW Summer Session and Winter Courses, and the Wyoming Engineering Society offer high school juniors an opportunity to participate in a summer program of hands-on experiences in a variety of engineering fields. Students participate in laboratory sessions, working one-on-one with faculty members and graduate students on projects such as building digital circuits or developing solutions to environmental problems.

University of Wyoming Summer High School Institute

Contact: Mr. Duncan Harris, Director

Address: Summer High School Institute
University of Wyoming
Red House Honors Center
200 S. 10th St.
Laramie, WY 82070

Phone: 307-766-3005

Fax: 307-766-4298

E-mail: hsi@uwyo.edu

Website: http://www.uwyo.edu/hsi

Program Type: Academic Enrichment

Grade/Age Levels: Grade 10

Description: The mission of the Summer High School Institute is to provide a place where some of the state's most intellectually talented sophomores can gather before their junior and senior years, living and studying in an environment with no pressure for grades, and sharing ideas and friendship with other gifted students. Students at this 3-week residential camp study courses such as Medications, Folk Tales, Exercise Physiology, Unraveling DNA, Hip-hop and Society, Robotic Engineering, and many other courses.

About the Author

Sandra L. Berger has been a citizen activist and advocate for gifted children for more than 30 years. She originally was led down this path by her own gifted youngsters. Berger holds a master's degree in gifted education curriculum and instruction with training in counseling. For 15 years, she was the gifted education information specialist at the ERIC Clearinghouse on Disabilities and Gifted Education and the AskERIC system, responding to thousands of questions about gifted and special education. She is a member of the editorial advisory board and a technology columnist for *Understanding Our Gifted*, has authored numerous articles in the field of gifted education, and shares her views on college planning and gifted education through participation in national, regional, and state conferences. Berger and her husband of 54 years currently have 5 grandchildren.